Praise for *Ge*

"After reading *Gender Balancing*, my thoughts traversed the years that my wife and I integrated the principles we absorbed from Martin's coaching. Our undisclosed secrets, unshared feelings, and unresolved issues are now small glimmers of our past. Martin's guidelines gave us tangible proof that a male and female bond can exist that is beyond the ordinary. We all have a secret desire to achieve complete happiness in our relationships without effort, and everything we need for that perfection needs no exertion if we let Martin's essence flow to fully get what we have been missing." —Dr. Alan Shader

"With his vibrant coaching and powerful distinctions about women and men, Martin inspires couples to create relationships more extraordinary than they could ever have imagined. He models the sensitivity, loving kindness, and playfulness that couples learn to integrate and cherish in their own relationships. A treasure trove of straight talk and practical wisdom, this book will benefit all who read it." —Dr. Ann B. Gordon, psychotherapist

"In reading *Gender Balancing*, I went through three emotional stages: intrigued, entertained, and profoundly moved. There were moments where I felt like Martin was inside my brain. It was a most pleasant surprise to find that Martin's words shifted my outlook on relationships. I had a very idealistic concept of love and men, which mostly came from movies, TV shows, and novels. *Gender Balancing* gave me a grounding view of who I am, and what kind of relationship I will create with my future partner/husband. I am grateful to have received this gift from Martin before getting into a relationship. I feel a clarity that allows me to be at peace with the circumstances of my love life, while at the same time creating a future that's way more exciting than my dreams! That's because I know I am creating something *real*." —Vanessa Lynn Uzcategui, TEFL educator and writer

"I love *Gender Balancing*! It is inspiring and absolutely brilliant in its simplicity and application. Martin takes the complication out of relationships. There is a playfulness about this book that places the reader realistically in how we live, love, and create. The cerebral aspects of love, commitment, and romance are rendered palatable for a tantalizing read. We should all immerse ourselves in this book; what we come away with is a fresh perspective on what it means to be in love. Martin has brought together those planetary aspects of our duality so that men and women occupy the same universe; regardless of the apparent illusion, we move and share as one." —Dr. Jim Valentine

"Martin's work on gender balancing and understanding relationship has had the deepest impact on my life, my relationships, and my ability to know what works and does not work in a relationship. He has empowered me as a woman, as a client, and as a professional partner, and he will always remain one of the people I trust most in my life. Martin's work is unique, his style is inimitable, and the depth of his heart and soul are evident in every word he writes or speaks. Martin's work in this book represents a remarkable synthesis of his lifetime commitment to discovering and presenting a new paradigm of possibility for relationships between women and men. Read it at your peril—once you *know* what relationship is all about, you can never go back to your old, familiar ways." —Dr. Mara Schiff, author and associate professor at Florida Atlantic University

"In *Gender Balancing*, I found a way to navigate the most difficult of human (mis)adventures. This book reflected my emotions, hesitations, and fear of commitment. From Martin's coaching, I have gained an understanding of myself. I am excited by his novel approach to gender balancing. I look forward to exploring what is waiting for me as I go through my transformation. I can only imagine living these principles. I want to change my relationships from mediocre to extraordinary! I can't wait to sit down and read *Gender Balancing* all over again. I am committed to altering my beliefs and continuing to work through closing the gap." —Alicia E. Quiroga, MD

"Here is your opportunity to get an expensive seminar for the cost of a book. This practical book will make an impact on every one of your relationships. Martin is an extraordinary coach who is in constant demand. What he does *works*. When I applied a single instruction from the introduction, my wife fell in love with me all over again." —Harvey W. Austin, MD, surgeon and author of *ELDERS ROCK!*

GENDER *Balancing*

An Evolutionary Model

for

Elevating Relationships

from

Mediocre to

EXTRAORDINARY

martin**CALDERON**COHEN

BALBOA.
PRESS

A DIVISION OF HAY HOUSE

Balboa Press books may be ordered through booksellers or by contacting:

Balboa Press
A Division of Hay House
1663 Liberty Drive
Bloomington, IN 47403
www.balboapress.com
1 (877) 407-4847

Because of the dynamic nature of the Internet, any web addresses or links contained in this book may have changed since publication and may no longer be valid. The views expressed in this work are solely those of the author and do not necessarily reflect the views of the publisher, and the publisher hereby disclaims any responsibility for them.

The author of this book does not dispense medical advice or prescribe the use of any technique as a form of treatment for physical, emotional, or medical problems without the advice of a physician, either directly or indirectly. The intent of the author is only to offer information of a general nature to help you in your quest for emotional and spiritual well-being. In the event you use any of the information in this book for yourself, which is your constitutional right, the author and the publisher assume no responsibility for your actions.

Any people depicted in stock imagery provided by Thinkstock are models, and such images are being used for illustrative purposes only.
Certain stock imagery © Thinkstock.

Print information available on the last page.

ISBN: 978-1-5043-3957-5 (sc)
ISBN: 978-1-5043-3959-9 (hc)
ISBN: 978-1-5043-3958-2 (e)

Library of Congress Control Number: 2015914550

Balboa Press rev. date: 09/29/2015

Contents

Foreword by Dr. Arthur Phillips ix

A Message from Martin xi

Introduction: Why This Book Is for You xv

SECTION 1—COACHING ORIENTATION

Chapter 1:   Powerful Baby Steps 3

Chapter 2:   An Ontological Perspective—Standing In the Future 7

Chapter 3:   What It Is to Be *Complete*—A New Beginning. 11

SECTION 2—THE GAP: FROM MEDIOCRE TO EXTRAORDINARY

Chapter 4:   Peace Among Women and Men 19

Chapter 5:   Relationships—Natural or Unnatural? 22

Chapter 6:   The Fundamental Differences Among Women and Men 28

Chapter 7:   What Women and Men Really *Want* and *Need* from Each Other. 32

Chapter 8:   Five Primary Relationships 37

Chapter 9:   Falling in Love Is Not Hard, but Staying in Love Is 48

Chapter 10: Deal Breakers for Committed Relationships 52

SECTION 3—GENDER BALANCING

Chapter 11: Genderless—Before Women and Men 59

Chapter 12: The Woman and Man Within You 61

Chapter 13: Discovering Your Feminine and Masculine Energies. . . . 63

Chapter 14: The Impact of Gender Imbalance 69

Chapter 15: An Ideal Balance of Feminine and Masculine Energies. . 75

SECTION 4—AN EVOLUTIONARY MODEL

Chapter 16: Communication: Your Pathway to Love 85

Chapter 17: Declaring Your Primary Commitments 88

Chapter 18: Creating a Power-Source Relationship. 90

Chapter 19: The Keys to Everlasting Love 94

Chapter 20: The New Model for Love 99

In Closing and Coaching 103

Acknowledgments 105

Foreword

Martin Cohen is a powerful motivational speaker and personal coach who has devoted his entire career to the empowerment of others and the fulfillment of their dreams. His passion for his work is always palpably present.

Although the discussion of gender dynamics has been a major topic of the past few decades, his work elevates the conversation to include the reality of the female and male attributes present in *all* people, both women and men, and the need for balance and harmony rather than victory. This is a message of new possibility for relationships with strong roots in the wisdom of the ancient past.

I recommend reading this book as though you were in the audience at one of Martin's workshops or in the privacy of a coaching session with him. The book is more than a discussion. It is specifically targeted so that something positive will happen within you.

What Martin Cohen does is bring about the actualization of the best in people.

Happier people make the world and their own lives better.

Arthur Phillips, MD
Author of *Transformational Psychotherapy*
Associate Clinical Professor of Psychiatry
UCSD, School of Medicine
San Diego, CA

A Message from Martin

In my early teens I heard the difference between male and female, and at first it made no sense. We were all speaking English, so how could this be? Why was the language so remarkably different? When I asked the boys I knew how they were doing, their responses came in short clips: fine, okay, not great, or a shrug with no response. When I asked the girls the same question, there would be a momentary pause and then a stream of conversation about school, friends, parents, boys, and other topics. In addition, they would complain about the things that bothered them.

The more I listened, the more intrigued I became. Why were their responses so different? Not only was I listening to what seemed like two distinct languages but what the boys and girls were communicating also had significantly different meanings. At some point, I decided to separate how I listened. I began to "change channels" internally when listening to females, and then I would "change channels" to listen to males. What I heard revealed a radical difference in who girls and boys were. I needed to dig deep down inside myself to understand so that I could assimilate their words and sounds from another context of communication. I would hear "female" internally; I would hear "male" externally. The boys' words spoke with pictures; the girls' words described their feelings. Based on who was speaking to me, I found myself continuously changing channels. It seemed confusing and illogical, yet I was fascinated. I wanted feedback on my discoveries. Was I crazy or was this real?

During a creative writing class in the ninth grade, I announced, "I believe the greatest untapped natural resource available to mankind is women!" The reaction was momentary silence followed by a burst of loud laughter. My teacher, Miss Port, ordered me to a corner and confronted me. What did I mean by that statement? I shared what I had discovered about the differences in the communication styles of boys and girls. She listened closely, and then she moved her face close to mine and said, "Martin, don't you ever stop!" I heard her words deep within, and I took them to heart; I have never stopped.

The phase of my life that followed was, for me, both obvious and astonishing. The more I explored the supposed differences between women and men, the better I understood this truth: there is a woman and man in each of us. Now, I do not mean this from a physical or a sexual perspective. What I mean is, the total energies that live inside us are expressed from opposing yet compatible energies. This is complicated but simple, and I will explain it to you in the book.

Once I understood this, the awareness left me with a deep commitment. I needed to research the conflict and understand the imbalance of the woman and man within me and within all of us. My mission in life crystallized. I followed the family tradition and began a career in the world of fashion. This was the platform that allowed me to further understand the respective energies of women and men. How women presented themselves in clothing, in an industry primarily run by men, further clarified the imbalance.

After twenty years in fashion, it was clear to me my life's mission was ready to be revealed. I began to develop myself by participating in transformational courses and programs. My natural expression as a coach and a leader emerged. I produced breakthrough results that made a difference in people's lives. I launched a coaching practice predominantly devoted to empowering relationships—from personal to business to corporate, in both the public and private sectors. The results I have seen from individual and group coaching have been immediate and life altering.

After working with a multitude of committed couples, I created a seminar I called "All About Men and Women." Modeled as an interactive discourse, the seminar revealed the gap that exists between mediocre relationships and our aspirations for extraordinary relationships. The gap is a wound we are experiencing, and the result is an epidemic of mediocre relationships. People are hurting, and they are left wanting.

There are very few role models for extraordinary relationships—relationships that empower and inspire others in relationships to be productive, creative, and satisfying, and that positively impact the community. We need to be taught how to change a mediocre relationship into an exciting one, how to have our relationships be extraordinary, and how to be in relationships that inspire others.

For more than three decades now, I have devoted my life to improving relationships. Through my coaching and seminars, I have made sure to spread the word, to share my understanding with as many people as possible. I have interacted with thousands of committed individuals, and we have produced breakthrough results. I have seen how moving from mediocre to extraordinary relationships will transform people's lives.

In this book I share with you the results of my decades of experience in the field of relationships. Here, I have taken a complicated subject and converted it into an easy-to-read and practical guide specifically designed to empower *your* committed relationships. If you wish to improve how you relate to your partner by embracing the woman and man within you, then your relationships will move from mediocre to extraordinary. Your life, too, will change.

Stay with it. This is what thousands of my clients have done, and it works!

Martin Calderon Cohen
www.martincohen.org

Introduction:
Why This Book Is for You

I believe that all human beings share a dream to have an amazing, fulfilling, and complete relationship with themselves and others. My life's mission is to make that dream come true.

For most people, the quest to find the right person, fall in love, and commit is challenging enough. Once we get into a relationship that has the potential to be that remarkable, fulfilling partnership we always dreamed of, most of us are clueless about how to make love last. That's why divorce rates are high and separations divide us. Many couples who do remain together find themselves in mediocre relationships; the relationships might be acceptable, but they fall far short of their hopes and dreams for what a relationship could be.

If your relationship is not living up to what you expected, that's not unusual; many people in committed relationships feel dissatisfaction. I know that because these people are my clients. It's my job to empower them—and to inspire you.

Those who come to me for coaching tend to be highly conscious people who are intent on living lives that are consistent with their dreams. My clients are committed to creating amazing lives and are open to discovering new possibilities to fulfill their goals. Highly conscious people desire exciting lives. Since you are reading this book, you are probably highly conscious as well.

Coaching will help uncover what is limiting you in the path to attaining your goals. Coaching will eliminate those obstacles and will also open up infinite possibilities for growth and development in your life, as well as in your relationships. My method of coaching comes from an ontological perspective. According to Webster's dictionary, ontology is "a branch of metaphysics dealing with the nature of being." [1] This is the study of who you are *being*, rather than what you are doing or what you have. Thus, my style of coaching brings your entire focus to your future. Most of the tools we use to examine ourselves come from a psychological perspective that uses the past to determine the present and the future. In contrast, the ontological perspective focuses on who you are being in the moment within the context of who you are committed to being in the future.

A great metaphor for the difference between psychology and ontology is to think of your life and everything that happens to you as a basket with apples in it. Psychology deals with the apples—the things that happened to you, the decisions you made, the minutiae, and your stories about your past. Ontology focuses exclusively on the basket as the context for your life and all that the basket contains. This allows for another perspective—it gives all the apples, including your relationships and your life, a context of unknown possibilities and meaning. This perspective allows you to explore a new realm for change, expanding your possibilities.

Coaching empowers my clients to close the gap in their relationships. They can move from where they are now to where they want to be. This book is intended to do the same for you. The focus for this book will be the primary relationship of a woman and a man who are committed but not fulfilled, but the underlying relationship you will be working on is the one with yourself—the relationship between the woman inside you and the man inside you, no matter which gender you may be.

I'm going to support you throughout the process in the same way

---

[1] *Merriam-Webster Dictionary Online*, s.v. "ontology," http://www.merriam-webster.com/dictionary/ontology

that I've supported thousands of individuals and couples across the country. *Gender Balancing* will teach you how to use the techniques I've developed to create and maintain deep levels of intimacy, love, and respect within your relationship. If you follow my program, the connection you have with your partner will transform from mediocre to extraordinary. Your relationship will be fulfilling and will likely last forever.

This is a coaching book. This means you must trust that, as your coach, I know the best for you and that I understand your limitations. I can see how you and your partner act and react in your relationship from a critically objective perspective. I can see what you are doing and how you are reacting more clearly than you are able to yourself. I am acting as your *coach*. Star athletes like LeBron James and Serena Williams wouldn't dream of going out on a court without the guidance of their coaches. Why? Because they understand that their coaches can see what the athletes themselves are blind to.

As your relationship coach, I'll point out *your* blind spots. I'll address where you may be stuck and what's going to change after you see yourself and your relationships from a new perspective. Seeing yourself from the outside is challenging, but as one of my clients says, "It may not always be easy, but Martin is always, always on your side." And that's true—throughout this book, I will always, always be on your side.

Within a year or two of being together as a couple, most partners believe they know one another, and they fall into a routine. This is natural. Commitment is different than the whirlwind of romance. Not only do you have to manage the day-in, day-out, practical needs of both yourself and your partner but you also begin to perceive the relationship differently. This happens once you have "declared" that you are committed to one another—whether you're married, living together, or seriously dating.

However, there are some significant differences in women and men that consistently cause conflicts in relationships. This is why they fail to meet each other's unspoken needs. I'll show you how to meet your partner's unspoken needs. Using illustrative stories from my decades of experience with clients, I will illustrate how doing so empowers both partners to extend themselves beyond what they receive. This removes the *quid pro quo* (or "I'll do as much for you as you are doing for me") dynamic from your relationship.

There are pitfalls in moving into the committed stage of a relationship. These can be at the root of the conflicts in a relationship. You can discover these by examining the conversations you have with yourself about your partner, as well as examining what you believe to be true about your partner. This will help you perceive your relationship from an objective point of view. It will support you in resolving conflicts and in avoiding them before they begin.

Throughout this book, you will examine the distinct differences among women and men. I say *among* rather than *between* because *among* represents women and men as total human beings, whereas *between* creates an opposing position. There is a mix of feminine and masculine energies in all human beings. It is your balance or imbalance of these energies that determines how you act in the world and how you communicate with the people in it. Your partner has his or her own balance of energies. The difference between your energy balance and your partner's affects how, and how well, you communicate with one another. If you've ever thought that your partner was "in his or her own world" or "speaking a different language," then you've experienced an imbalance in these energies in your relationship.

An important topic is how to be "safe" for your partner. I'll also define what is essential for your relationship to flourish and explain how to communicate that to your partner so that you will live happily ever after.

Consider the possibility that you may have no idea what a committed, loving relationship is. I say this because I see it so often with my clients. We think we know what a loving relationship entails, but we are often misguided. The more you can suspend your belief that you already know about relationships, the more effective my coaching will be for you. This means you will read this book with a beginner's mind, which requires that you let relationships have a mystery that can't quite be solved. This is an opportunity for you to start from the beginning, to start from a place of "I don't know."

The coaching in this book will elevate the relationship you have now, the one you've settled for. The material and the techniques you learn will bring you infinitely closer to what you dreamed your love life or your marriage would be. You will be empowered, and you will deeply understand who you are—in relationships and in your own being.

The dream still resides within your heart. You have what it takes to make it come true.

Notes to Myself

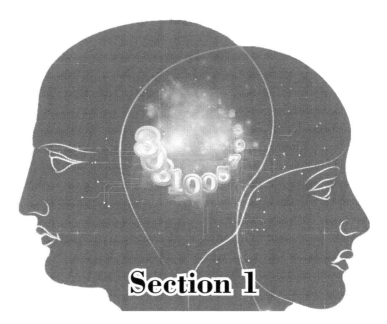

Section 1

Coaching Orientation

Chapter 1:
Powerful Baby Steps

You might be thinking, *Who is this Martin Cohen? Why should I trust him when I've been trying so hard and nothing has changed?* All my clients think this way. But then we move ahead, and their lives begin to shift.

In our first meeting, I request of my clients the following: they must generate a new action and take a powerful baby step. This demonstrates the possibility of transforming their relationships by using my coaching guidelines. If they cannot take the baby step, the journey will not proceed. For you, taking a baby step will help you to see how far you can go with the guidelines provided in this book. Take the baby step.

If you decide this doesn't work for you, that's your choice. You can put the book down, complain about it at your local bookstore, ship it back to Amazon, delete it from your tablet, or dump it in the trash. But if you do choose to take the powerful baby step, your life will change. You will noticeably alter how your partner relates to you. I've seen my clients' relationships transform almost instantly in front of me. In mere minutes! The baby step is *that* powerful.

Your First Baby Step

You can take this first powerful baby step on your own. Typically, I recommend that clients do it without telling their partners. That way they will see the shift in their dynamic as a couple without the possibility that it is merely a placebo effect. If you want to tell your partner after you see the shift, then this works as a good way to announce that you are being coached.

So, here's your baby step. For the next week, look for opportunities to *authentically acknowledge* your partner. What I mean by this is to verbally recognize and confirm her or his specific contributions to your relationship. You may acknowledge anything you like, from physical tasks like taking out the trash or cooking dinner to more emotional contributions like actively listening or contributing to a discussion of your day.

If he smiles at you in a way you like, tell him you like it. If she offers to buy dinner, say, "I appreciate that. Great. Thank you." Once you change the way you relate to your partner, she or he will respond in kind. Your interactions will stand out and your communications will be different from what you have established as your pattern.

A crucial part of this baby step is that you *not* use it as a technique. Your partner will pick up on any attempt at manipulation, so don't try too hard. If you make a conscious effort to observe the little things that happen between you, you will notice plenty of opportunities to authentically acknowledge your partner. When you find one, say something. Then sit back and observe the response.

This baby step is powerful because when a man feels authentically acknowledged, he feels empowered to take care of his woman—not only to take care of her, but to take *great* care of her—and when a woman feels authentically acknowledged, she experiences being known and profoundly respected. Your partner may increase how often he holds your hand in public, or she may want to be intimate more often when you're in private. She may show you more affection; he may treat you with greater respect. When you authentically acknowledge your partner on a consistent basis, *you* experience being profoundly respected. This is because when your partner feels acknowledged and taken care of, you will experience being respected.

This simple baby step—offering authentic acknowledgment for a week—will lead to greater appreciation. The appreciation will be felt by both of you, and this will create a snowball effect. The positive results will continuc to expand. After taking your first baby step, you may be encouraged by the results. However, you will most likely still feel that having an extraordinary relationship with your partner is a long shot, a far off dream that might never come true. Most of my clients feel this way in the beginning, but if you are open to not knowing everything and open to the coaching in this book, you *will* have the transformation in your relationship that you desire. You might not believe it right now, but soon enough you will see even more incredible results. Then you will be certain.

Take Another Step

Maybe you had terrific results with the first baby step and want to attempt another one. Or perhaps the reaction you saw from your partner was just so-so, and you're not quite convinced my coaching will work for you. Either way, the second baby step is important. Take this step and you will be amazed at the results. The next time you and your partner begin to argue about something, see if you can change what you say into a request. Instead of saying, "I don't really like it when …" or "I hate it when …" or "You drive me nuts when …" you can say, "Would you mind if I made a request? You don't have to accept it, but I'd appreciate it if you would …"

Most of us are used to arguing. We're used to the pinball game of going back and forth with words. We say something we know will trigger a reaction, and then we watch that reaction, which in turn escalates our partner's reaction. Pretty soon we're throwing tantrums or taking ourselves away, refusing to speak to one another or exploding and saying unforgivably hurtful things.

When you make a request, it stops the pinball game. A request makes the other person stop yelling and stop being defensive because she or he needs to think. This forces the other person to engage with the question and the request, which stops the argument and begins a new conversation. That doesn't necessarily mean the fight will be resolved, because your request can always be denied, but it does mean you'll stop yelling. That's a good start to resolving any conflict.

You can try this with a knock-down, drag-out fight, a screaming match, or a little disagreement. You can use it as a way to discuss pesky habits that bug you. For example, say a loving couple—Bob and Linda—is in the middle of a nasty argument. Both are insistent they are right about their respective opinions. Then Linda stops arguing midstream, looks directly at her partner, and says, "Bob, I have a request for you. Would you please share with me what you think my point of view is in this argument?" Bob immediately stops speaking and begins to think about what Linda has been saying. He proceeds to tell her what he believes she was attempting to communicate.

There is a visible shift that comes over Bob in directing Linda's communication back to her. An instantaneous phenomenon has just occurred. Bob has entered into Linda's world. What follows is this: Linda reflects Bob's point of view. Bob is touched that Linda understands him so deeply. Their argument no longer exists! An opening for the loving commitment they have for each other is all that is present. The request is what caused a breakthrough in their relationship.

So use Linda and Bob's technique next time you have an opportunity. Every argument, disagreement, or annoying habit is another chance for communication, a way to achieve a breakthrough in your relationship. Both of these baby steps will support you in taking giant steps on your path to that dream-come-true relationship.

Chapter 2:
An Ontological Perspective—
Standing In the Future

Over the past thirty years, I've heard a lot of secondhand advice—the kind received by my clients about relationships. Wow. There's a lot of misinformed advice out there! The advice you may get from friends is mostly talk; there is no solution there. It may make you feel better at the time, but following the advice does not improve the relationship. That's because most conventional relationship advice focuses on fixing problems caused by past history or issues. Those approaches are faulty because both the history and the issues were inadvertently created.

In reality, there's no reason to bring your past into your present, much less your future. Our culture has given those psychological concepts—the things that happened in our past—way too much power and prominence. When a relationship isn't living up to all it could be, it is easy to label that a problem and to try to fix it, but the reason that approach doesn't create the kind of change you intend is that it's fundamentally impossible to change another person unless the other person is completely on board with the change and the method.

With my clients, I focus on their commitment to the future. My approach is based on an ontological perspective—that is, the intentional focus is on who you are *being* rather than on what you *do* or what you *have.* It can be helpful to think of ontology as anything but ordinary thinking. In psychology, the past directly impacts the present. It's as if you are standing in the past while breathing in the present. In ontology, we begin with the future, as if you are standing in the future while breathing in the present; that has the potential for breakthrough. We create a new future by defining what we are committed to and then using that as the measure for our behavior and decisions in present time.

It is essential for you to creatively design your future as a reality—that is, to imagine your future as specifically as possible. This means you must use all of your five senses; imagine what you will see, touch, hear, smell, and taste. This will give you the most potent experience of standing with both your feet in your future. In doing so, you are creating your future as a living reality.

You are now ready to transport yourself to present time. Ask yourself the following questions: Are you being a leader in this moment? Are you, in this moment, open to possibility? Are you being positive, empathetic, generous, and transparent, or are you being negative, conflicted, angry, frustrated, and passive? How does the way you are being in this moment influence your goals, dreams, and visions for the future?

Let's examine an ontological example: Have you ever wondered what it is like to *be,* or what *being* is like, for a person of the opposite gender? Can you imagine what is it like to actually experience *being* your partner?

If we consciously evaluate how we are *being*, then we can connect that to what we aspire to for our future and work toward that end. Let's suppose your goal is to be a caring spouse. Declare that out loud to yourself: "I am a caring spouse." Do this on a regular basis so you will be conscious of that declaration in your daily life. After you do this, what you are doing will either lead to or challenge you in realizing this outcome. What you accomplish will emanate from being a caring spouse.

An ontological approach does not attempt to change your partner or her or his behavior. It illuminates another perspective. Instead of trying to fix a single problem or an issue, you shift your perspective. You take a futuristic approach to your relationship, which transforms the dynamic between you and your partner.

Ask yourself the following question: how would you describe your integrity in your past and present relationships? When I say your integrity, I'm specifically pointing to the times that you did not do what you knew was expected of you. This includes when you did not keep your word when you had agreed to. The predictable response to this question is "I'm hurt, angry, embarrassed, and ashamed."

Now ask yourself this question: how would you describe your integrity in your relationships in the future? My clients typically respond with confidence, "My future integrity is impeccable and flawless! I feel free and light, no longer burdened!"

At the point that you envision having integrity in your relationship in the future, you will no longer be encumbered by your past integrity. What I mean by integrity is simply the commitment to honor your word as the essence of who you are. In your declaration of being extraordinary, your relationship to integrity affects all aspects of your workability, performance, and results.

Declaring how you are being (in this case, being a caring partner) in the moment creates an unknown future. That unknown future is completely in sync with who you've declared yourself to be and what you've declared you are committed to—that is, to having an extraordinary relationship. It's as if you are looking back from the future to present time.

The ontological perspective opens up infinite possibilities in our lives and our relationships, regardless of our behavior in the past. All that it requires is that you take a powerful stand for the future you declare and live in a way that moves you into that reality. It's okay if you don't fully understand ontology after reading this chapter. Ontology is easier to understand in action than from reading about it. As you begin to practice these new actions, you will come to a greater understanding of the process. The key point for you right now is this: your past is no longer meaningful in relation to what you are creating for your future.

Chapter 3:
What It Is to Be *Complete*—
A New Beginning

What we call the beginning is often the end. And
to make an end is to make a beginning.

—T.S. Eliot

Being complete is one of life's greatest challenges and cannot easily be explained. It is a phenomenon that occurs in language and in action. What does it mean to be complete? It means being whole, lacking nothing, and accepting yourself, others, and all your circumstances exactly the way they are. Being complete begins and ends with a bold declaration and does not mean "finished or over." Through your declaration of being complete, it closes that chapter of your life in a way that allows for a new opening.

The need to declare yourself complete is not limited to dealing with negative events or people. You may also declare yourself complete regarding accomplishments, breakthroughs, and other specific life experiences. Being complete emanates from language, and is generated by your word. The power of declaring oneself complete causes a finality that uncovers a vision or reality that would not have happened had you not declared yourself complete.

The fear of or resistance to declaring yourself complete perpetuates any aspect of your history that has been limiting you. If you indulge such memories or stories from your past, repeating them in a negative internal conversation, you will reinforce that conversation. This is not what you want, even if you enjoy repeating your old stories to yourself.

The existential act of declaring yourself complete not only closes the door but also locks it and throws away the key, leaving you with *nothing*. This will have that limitation that was previously so integral to your life disappear. You will then be left with a clear space to create what's next for you. A new door—a door to the unknown—is there for you to open. The internal conversation you were having for so long had an energy of its own. Completing this aspect of your life releases that energy. This takes courage. Consider this act a brave choice, one you are making in order to face your next life challenge magnificently.

The completion exercise below will help you to take this step. You are choosing to enter into the next realm of possibility for your life. The commitment to being complete can be communicated to yourself as you make this commitment alone. You can also choose to share it with someone else or with a group of individuals aligned to similar life changes.

Completion as a way of life is an invaluable perspective. To live this way is to take a step toward living your life more fully, at the same time creating your new future *now*. Once you are established in your life's commitment to being complete, you will have given yourself a life-altering gift.

Completion Exercise: Becoming Complete with Your Parents

Step 1:

Speak about your relationship with your mother or father. Speak of it to yourself or with a trusted family member, friend, or peer. There's no need to break it down, relive the emotions from the past, or justify your feelings or behavior. Speak about what you are troubled by as clearly and plainly as you can. Speak with the intention to be complete.

Step 2:

Answer the following question, but limit your answer to either *yes* or *no*:

Do you have the capacity and the capability, despite whatever has happened in the past with your mother or father, to declare "I am complete with [your mother or father] unconditionally and absolutely, which means that I have affinity with and respect for [her or him] whether we agree or disagree, both in the present and the past"?

If you answered yes, then move on to step 3. If you answered no, take some additional time to speak about or write down your thoughts and feelings. If you begin expressing yourself, step 1 can become effective and authentic.

Step 3:

Speak the following out loud:

"I declare I am complete with [your mother or father] unconditionally and absolutely. What I mean by *complete* is that I have an affinity with and respect for [your mother or father] regardless of whether I agree or disagree with [her or him] about what happened in the past, what's happening in the present, and what may happen in the future."

It may take time for you to express your incompletions about the past and the present, as well as to acknowledge your fears about the future. Once you are able to declare yourself complete, however, the declaration will open up a vast space of possibility for you and others. You'll be able to discuss your relationships without the tension. You will be able to empathetically complete issues in the past that remain unresolved for others, too, which will immediately improve your relationships with them.

Becoming complete with your parents empowers you in the present, which will support you in your work to improve your relationship with your partner, both in the present and the future. Your relationship with your parents impacts the foundation of your success in relationships with others. Your relationship with family influences your overall success at relationships and your level of happiness throughout your life.

My client Margaret was divorced. She's an attractive woman in her forties, and she's a successful executive. Margaret's primary commitments in our coaching sessions were to be in a happy, productive, and compatible relationship with a man who met her standards and to build a family. However, her history of being in relationships with men, including the man she was briefly married to, was one of anger, complicated by ongoing arguments and struggles. Yet Margaret was sure she did not want to grow old alone. Her fear of such a future was affecting the overall quality of her life.

Margaret's relationship with her father became the focus of our discussions. She described him as an angry man—cynical, righteous, and highly critical of everyone around him. This included Margaret, her mother, her brother, her sister, and even their friends. Growing up was a battle for survival. She struggled to keep her head above water. Developing lasting friendships seemed impossible.

Margaret needed to work on being complete with those past relationships. Reaching completion moved her forward as she understood her father as the first man in her life, a "sourced relationship" that impacted her future relationships with men. Once she understood that her father had been incapable of being any other way than the way he was, she felt liberated. She recalled making a decision in her early teens to never let herself be hurt by a man. After her realizations were crystalized, Margaret moved ahead. She stated, "I declare myself unconditionally complete with my father!"

Her intention in that declaration was powerful, real, resolute, and complete. After she made her declaration, I saw an immediate shift in her demeanor. With tears in her eyes, she began speaking with empathy for her father. She forgave him. She then forgave herself for all the negative thoughts and feelings she had directed toward him over the years. This led Margaret to declare herself complete with all men. Margaret chose to actively develop a new relationship with her father. She shared her breakthrough with her family. Her transformation served as an inspiration that transformed the unity of Margaret's family. Since then, the quality of Margaret's life has dramatically altered. She met the man of her dreams and married him. Together they adopted two children.

Such is the power of being complete.

Notes to Myself

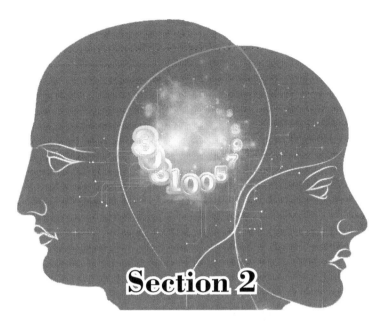

Section 2

The Gap: From Mediocre
to Extraordinary

Chapter 4:
Peace Among Women and Men

Has the historical conflict that exists among women and men ever truly been explored?

Clearly the conflict could be considered an unspoken conspiracy that exists in all cultures living on the planet. Sometimes the war is barely discernible or recognizable; other times it is dramatically and radically obvious. This unspoken conflict has evolved inside a "condition of patriarchy."

"Patriarchy is a social arrangement in which males hold more social, economic and political power compared to females. It refers to a society in which power is disproportionately held by men. Patriarchy is not in our genes or part of biology instead it is a social construct which can be seen as part of our cultural belief system."[2]

During a speech in 2003, Joan Holmes, founding president and CEO of The Hunger Project spoke about the condition of patriarchy.

● ●

> What I refer to is patriarchy—a universal mind-set that has been in existence since the dawn of civilization. Our behavior as women in the developed world is as much an adaptation to that system as is men's behavior.

[2] "Patriarchy," *Anthropology & the Human Condition*, last modified October 18, 2010, http://sc2218.wikifoundry.com/page/Patriarchy.

● ●

In our struggle as women to achieve equality and be fully expressed human beings, if we see the struggle as between genders, then we actually reinforce and validate the patriarchic mind-set.

Instead, if we as women say, "Let's look at the adaptations we've had to make within the system of patriarchy, and see what we need to do to transform our way of being," then we will not be accommodating patriarchy, we'll be catalyzing its transformation.

It's important to identify the beliefs inherent in patriarchy.

The beliefs about women are that they are incapable, incompetent, weak, untrustworthy, of less value than men, and need to be controlled and dominated.

The beliefs regarding men are that they are competent, able, strong, rational, not emotional, of more value than women, and that they have a God-given mandate to control, be in charge and dominate.

What are the consequences of buying into those beliefs?

For a woman to buy into, "I'm incompetent, submissive and of less value" is to not be fully realized as a human being. And for men to buy into "I'm better, more competent and more valuable," when there is overwhelming evidence to the contrary, is to live a lie, and therefore to live a distorted and dehumanizing existence.

With this recognition, we start to understand—not condone, but understand—that if you have that big a lie on the planet for so many years, the only way you can keep it in place is by violence or the threat of violence. And we need to recognize that the greatest human rights violation on the planet today is violence against women.

No one is winning within the universal mind-set of patriarchy. Women are leading confined, distorted, shrunken lives, and so are men. Men are just doing it with more power.[3]

....

This is the time to generate a critical mass of highly committed women and men to align themselves on the creation of a declaration of peace among women and men. This declaration, powerfully spoken around the world, would be something to live into. It would call for the alignment of world leaders who are creating the doctrines, structures, and educational systems and would focus on manifesting itself into existence on the world agenda. There would be a focus on youth and future generations. This declaration enables the creation of a new paradigm. It is essential that this declaration be accelerated with urgency and initiated with immediacy in every country.

---

[3] Joan Holmes, "Women and Philanthropy: The Condition of Patriarchy," (speech delivered December 2003, Bangladesh).
....

Chapter 5:
Relationships—Natural or Unnatural?

To say that relationships are natural is to set yourself up for unfulfilled expectations. Relationships do not come naturally to us because we are all different. Not only are two individuals not the same but the closer they get as a couple, the more apparent their differences become. However, what *is* natural and shared is our likenesses as human beings.

Priority influences have a powerful and often indelible impact on the shaping of one's life and relationships. These influences include history, culture, family, tragedies, education, physicality, upbringing, economics, community, beliefs, and lifestyle. In any couple, there is at least one difference among these priority influences between the two individuals. The partners do not share the same histories, families, or upbringing. They may come from different cultures or communities and have different beliefs. They may come from divergent economic backgrounds or lifestyles and have different educations. They are physically different.

With all these differences, an eventual breakdown is predictable. The common adage that opposites attract can be true at first glance. Yet over time, the foundation of each person's priority influences will move to the forefront, and the initial attraction will move to the background. This is not always the case, but too often this is exactly what does occur.

Within the existing culture, freedom of expression and the ability to be uniquely yourself is revealing new forms of relationships. There are new definitions for committed relationships and marriage. Traditional marriages have declined proportionally over time, but the divorce rate has remained at around 50 percent. The divorce rate in couples over the age of fifty who have been married fifteen years or longer has doubled in the past twenty years.[4] Successful relationships that continue to grow do exist. In such relationships, the partners have developed loving perspectives that allow them to consistently embrace their differences. This usually includes the ability to laugh and joke about their differences.

Committed relationships and marriages may not be the best or healthiest choice for all individuals. Clearly the number of people who choose to remain in committed relationships seems to decline over time. We believe it is natural to cohabitate, grow and evolve, and to be committed to another human being. We think if we find someone who is our ideal match, this will be easy to do. However, this is not necessarily so. Living together creates the need for compromise, sacrifice, and acceptance of the other. People change over time, and it can get increasingly difficult for couples to do what they must to maintain their relationships. Being a couple magnifies your differences. Small things seem larger than they are. This perspective seems to create less space, limiting an individual's natural ability to be fully self-expressed. This leads to the individuals in a couple attempting to change themselves or, more often, their partners.

---

[4] Marriage and Divorce rates: Bureau of Labor Statistics, "Marriage and divorce: patterns by gender, race, and educational attainment," http://www.bls.gov/opub/mlr/2013/article/marriage-and-divorce-patterns-by-gender-race-and-educational-attainment.htm; Stevenson and Wolfers, "Marriage and Divorce: Changes and Their Driving Forces," Journal of Economic Perspectives 21(2) (Spring 2007), pp. 27-52; Sam Roberts, "Divorce after 50 Grows More Common," *New York Times*, September 20, 2013, http://www.nytimes.com/2013/09/22/fashion/weddings/divorce-after-50-grows-more-common.html?_r=0; Tracy Moore, "That 50 Percent Divorce Statistic Hasn't Been True For a Long Time," Jezebel, December 4, 2014, http://jezebel.com/that-50-percent-divorce-statistic-hasnt-been-true-for-a-1665833364.

Historically, the relationships between women and men were designed to provide each with protection, shelter, and food. Over time, this evolved to a socio-economic union, since it is cheaper to live in pairs than alone. These days, none of this may factor into the choice to be a couple. Modern couples are creating and customizing committed relationships with conditions and agreements that support both parties. This may be closer to what it takes for human beings to create a new paradigm for committed relationships.

Superstitions as Beliefs

Where did our superstitions come from? Where did our beliefs originate? Think about this. So much of what we believe has been invented—made up by someone—then spoken often enough over time that the ideas gained power. So much of what we believe is simply *not true.*

Changing your relationship and your life requires that you be bold enough to question your beliefs about women, men, and relationships. Your beliefs may be limiting you. Question them, challenge them, and then objectively evaluate whether you have been empowered by these beliefs. If you are empowered by a belief, keep it. If you are not empowered by the belief, give it up. Create your own belief instead.

What would work for you in your current or future relationship? What you believe has an enormous impact on you and your relationships. Be wise about what you take for granted as the truth. Here is a small sample of the many widely held beliefs that so many people in our culture believe to be "truths":

- Marriage is natural.
- Love is forever.
- Your soul mate exists.
- Love is the answer.
- Relationships are hard work.

- There is something wrong with you if you're not in a relationship.
- You can change your partner.
- Your relationship can only get better.
- Romance is forever.
- When a relationship ends, it is one person's fault.
- You need love for a successful marriage.
- Men are immature.
- Women are emotional.
- There is a scarcity of good men.
- Women are complicated.

It is important to realize that superstitions and beliefs have all been made up by people. These superstitions and beliefs have long been spoken as the truth in a way that has influenced cultures. At the moment that these superstitions and beliefs came to be considered true, alternative ideas or beliefs became virtually impossible to realize. The impact of giving power to these superstitions and beliefs is great. It has been damaging and limiting.

One example of a superstition or belief that was once accepted as true was the belief in witchcraft. Thousands of people, mostly women, were accused of being witches in the seventeenth century. In some places, practicing witchcraft was deemed punishable by death. The accused were tortured, drowned, hanged, or burned at the stake. Their persecution was a product of the belief that using intuition or alternative medicine constituted satanic cultism. These beliefs were superstitions; they were wrong, yet they swept vast geographical areas and had unnecessary and fatal results.

Beliefs and superstitions about relationships have developed credibility that can prevent a potential loving relationship from flourishing. By giving power to these beliefs, you are unable to see the truth. You are unable to trust your own experience about what you need and what best supports you.

Perhaps "witches" were expressing their unique ability to envision the future and too many men were resistant to the futuristic perspective that many women innately possess. For many men, there is an unspoken fear that a woman might envision a future that appears illogical and nonsensical. This then is perceived as a threat.

When Caroline came for coaching, she was exhausted from trying to find a partner. She was in her mid-thirties and wanted to start a family. Her fear was that there was no man who was right for her, so there would be no family. Caroline strongly believed there was a scarcity of good men who could qualify to be her life partner. This belief affected her life choices. She became so desperate for companionship that she began dating married men. This felt better to her than being alone. Married men seemed to care for her more than the single men she had been in relationships with.

The key in our coaching was for her to see her pattern. She needed to determine what was predictable and understand that each relationship would end, once again leaving her alone. My coaching helped her to let go of her need to be in a relationship. Any relationship. The "wrong" relationships.

Caroline stopped dating. Her focus shifted to loving and respecting herself powerfully. She began to see that because she was not loving and respecting herself, the men she attracted were not loving or respecting her either. Caroline realized that the cost to her aliveness, health, and wellness far exceeded any benefit she was experiencing from being with someone. By giving up her attachment to being with a man, she began to experience love and respect for herself. There was an obvious shift in how she perceived herself. This attracted men to Caroline who were seeking the kind of woman she was.

A few months into her coaching, Caroline began dating again. This happened without her actively looking for a partner. The wave of upstanding men of character who flooded into her life created a new dilemma. There were more men who she found attractive and who were attracted to her than she had time for!

The breakthrough happened. After giving up looking for her man, her man found her. She accepted a heartfelt proposal and is now happily married and creating a family with the man she loves.

Chapter 6:
The Fundamental Differences Among Women and Men

W omen and men are not the same physically. They tend to look different, and people tend to experience a magnetic attraction to what is different from themselves. We are attracted to individuals who do not have the same face, eyes, body shape, size, or strength.

In my experience of working with thousands of women and men over more than three decades, I have found that people are equally attracted by the differences that are not visible. One such difference is that women tend to have a connection to the future that is totally innate, while for men, the singular and solitary focus is on the present.

Let me explain what I have seen and experienced in working with my clients. A woman's relationship to her integrity—that is, what she perceives as right or wrong and acceptable or unacceptable—is highly sensitized. Her relationship to integrity includes the manner in which she speaks and listens. Her interpretation may be closer to the truth. This perspective allows her to manage, create, and monitor multiple aspects of what is vital to build and develop. Including situational events, campaigns, and strategies because she has a discerning eye on the future. This innate characteristic combines integrity with an ability to see and create the future. Because of this, women can be an invaluable resource in moving forward toward a new paradigm for relationship.

Conversely, the man in present time tends to have the capacity and capability to generate. He can build *her* vision into the physical universe. His expertise can border on a brilliant art form that creates the existence of the linear world.

The marriage and partnership of these inherent differences can be equated to a harmonious dance. This dance can create the foundation for a world that works for everyone and leaves nobody out.

The differences among women and men are obvious in certain areas. However, these differences are generalizations, and I use them here to illustrate my points.

For example, a woman's memory of being hurt may develop into a "scorecard" that can be readily accessed. It will take into consideration her relationship to the past and how she utilizes it in the present or at a future time. Her relationship to commitment is powerful and far-reaching. A man's commitment, however, tends to exist powerfully in the present. Thus the commitment may easily dissipate or disappear at some point in his future. When he spoke it originally, it was real for him. Yet over time, the power of that commitment may cease to be what it once was. The commitment may lose its meaning. Of course, this is not always the case.

If we confront the differences among women and men, we can begin to see the extraordinary similarity we have as human beings. When we can observe and embrace our respective differences, extraordinary relationships will evolve. Such relationships will then become the norm instead of the predominantly mediocre and ordinary relationships that currently make our lives so unsatisfying.

The Unique Strengths of a Woman and a Man

A man's perspective on relationships is usually not the same as a woman's. The strength and power of the man comes from the perspective that his reality is located in present time. Whatever he's saying in any given moment may not exist into the future. This does not mean he is intentionally lying; it just means the future doesn't naturally occur to him. What a man says and experiences in any given moment is totally real to him and is powerful unto itself. When a man professes love or commitment, he is highly trustworthy. This is because he's focused and intentional in making those statements. In other words, he's being a romantic. However, it is important to know that what a man says and speaks in that moment doesn't always occur to him as necessarily containing a depth or power that relates to the future.

While the power of a man is in his statement said in the moment, the power of a woman is in her profound experiences and statements expressed over time. When she comes home to her man, she sees herself with that man indefinitely, perhaps forever. There is always an aspect of the woman's world that includes her man. He is always present in her world, albeit at different levels. A man doesn't always include a woman in his world when he physically leaves her presence.

Even the meaning of commitment is different for each of them. For the woman, it's inclusive—the man is always with her. For the man, though he might remember his wife or his relationship, he truly isn't with her unless she's present and physically with him; this correlates to his focus being primarily about himself in the moment. This does not mean, however, that he does not love her; nor does it mean that the man doesn't believe in the commitment or that the relationship is in trouble. This is simply a difference among women and men—one that has implications for committed relationships.

Jessica told me her husband did not understand her and could not follow her conversations. This created a breakdown in their ability to share with each other. The frustration they both felt had led to anger and nasty arguments.

My coaching to Jessica was as follows: "You are speaking simultaneously from your past, present, and future. Your husband is listening from the present only. What you are saying is confusing to him."

Jessica looked surprised. She said, "I don't know. Let me ask him if that's true."

Her husband confirmed what I had told her. In that moment, Jessica saw the simplicity of his perspective. This changed her own view on communicating with him.

She began to practice speaking and requesting precisely what she wanted him to understand. She specifically spoke to the bottom line. Their conversations improved dramatically, and the connection they both felt restored their love and affinity.

Chapter 7:

What Women and Men Really *Want* and *Need* from Each Other

As a relationship coach, I've worked with many different people—women and men; single people and married people; young adults, octogenarians, and those in between. I have come to certain conclusions based on my own observations. Here is what I have found to be true: In order to be in a healthy relationship, it is essential to understand what the other person might expect or desire from you. This may sound simple, but you would be surprised how many people just do not understand this.

Although every individual is different, there are four major principles regarding what women and men require from each other. We will first look at what women want and need, then at what men want and need.

What Women Want and Need from Men

1. To Be Fun

The fun that men may innately embody has a childlike quality. It is fundamentally light, carefree, naïve, and in the moment. This kind of fun is uncomplicated and unhindered by thought, and it contains an adorable quality that goes beyond what could be planned or intentional. For many women, being with a man like this can be a breath of fresh air. It is also grounding, as in its presence, women need not think about anything other than enjoying, appreciating, and laughing. This could be considered the antithesis of how a woman's mind tends to work.

2. To Be Certain and Clear

Certainty and clarity are often significant challenges for men because they tend not to be able to provide them. To meet expectations, a man would have to address a woman with a concise, powerful approach that is not dominating or aggressive. When opinions or directions are spoken with certainty and clarity within the context of love and respect, the woman is relieved of the pressure to analyze. She is empowered not to have to take the lead.

3. To Be a Lover and Generator

A woman may dream of being pursued and loved by a man who is a hopeless romantic, generating for her the love and intimacy she wants him to want as well. His pursuit is physical, intentional, and filled with words of everlasting love. The woman's capacity to receive love is infinite; the man's role is to fulfill as much of that as possible.

4. To Be Profoundly Respectful: The Context

It is essential for men to uphold profound respect at all times in a relationship with a beloved woman. Profound respect directly correlates to the woman's experience of being loved completely. Profound respect deeply honors the woman in all aspects, situations, and scenarios from opening her door to smiling at her to acknowledging her. This kind of respect borders on a reverence that speaks to her as a remarkable woman, resource, treasure, and possibly mother and friend. What is essential inside of this profound respect is the total willingness to extend oneself as a privilege.

What Men Want and Need from Women

1. To Be Safe

The principal of safety is essential in creating a successful, powerful, and happy long-standing relationship. This requires a woman to know that the man is different and is *not her*. Thus, the woman's intention would be to create the possibility for the man to be totally *himself* in all ways possible. This includes his greatness and the child within him, his brilliance, his simplicity, his creativity, his foolishness and his young soul, that which a woman may love, and that which seems so illogical, making no sense whatsoever.

For the man to regard the woman as "safe," she must create space for him to be who he is. Doing so is an altruistic gift the woman simultaneously gives to herself and to him. This gift will give rise to countless and perhaps infinite realized possibilities beyond logical comprehension. The woman's courage comes in the face of the awareness that there is no guarantee about the couple's future together. Being safe demonstrates a woman's unconditional love and her commitment to creating an extraordinary relationship. When a woman is not safe; the man's predictable reaction is to limit being fun, certain and clear, and a lover and generator with the woman. The impact on her and their relationship is often harmful.

2. To Be Visionary

A woman exercising her innate ability to envision the future in the best way possible makes a man happy. A woman has the capacity and creativity to create a picture that allows the man to see the future *now*. From the man's perspective, this borders on psychic. Most men cannot do this, many women can. This vision allows the woman to cause a future that previously did not seem possible. This futuristic gift is natural to the essence of who women tend to be. What is required of the woman is to give herself permission to look deeply and to trust her timeless existence, so that she can express what she sees that brings the future to life.

This visionary muscle, fully exercised and spoken, is magically potent. When accompanied by actions, conversations, and structure to fulfill that vision, the result is an aligned vision that leaves an inspirational impact and creates a future to live into.

3. To Be Fulfilled and Complete as a Woman

There is no register or litmus test measuring the degree that you may love and respect yourself. However, you may not have adequate love and respect for yourself at all times. If you look deeply, there are times when love and respect for yourself is virtually nonexistent.

Women more often than men tend to lack adequate self-love and respect. However, being fulfilled and complete as a woman will take her out of the game when it comes to being attached to having a committed relationship. She will no longer be attached to the assumption that she *must* be in a committed relationship with a man. Not being attached allows her the freedom to powerfully choose to be or not to be in a relationship. This does not mean, though, that she does not love and appreciate being in relationship.

It is essential for women to be responsibly conscious that they possess the indomitable right to choose. Women can choose to be in a committed relationship or not. If she does choose to be in a committed relationship and is already fulfilled and complete as a woman, she will instantly create a demand for her from the man. He will pursue and love her as the woman of his choice.

4. To Give Authentic Acknowledgment: The Context

Building and creating inside the physical universe is an omnipotent exercise. Creating something from nothing is not easy. It may require physical effort, an art, and a skill, as well as the intention to bring to life a tangible creation. Building and creating can require overcoming limitations and what may appear to be insurmountable challenges.

When a man is building, it is essential for the woman to authentically acknowledge what he creates as a completion and as an impetus to live into a new future. The woman's honest acknowledgment speaks to the man through a loving approach that powerfully supports all he has created and all that he is committed to building; it makes his unique contribution worthwhile. When this happens, women and men are equally empowered within the relationship.

When a woman and man provide what they want and need from each other fully, their relationship will move beyond mediocre to extraordinary. Each partner has an overall experience of her or his own greatness, having it all with nothing left out or missing. I have seen this happen countless times. It really works.

Chapter 8:
Five Primary Relationships

You may experience at least five primary relationships over your lifetime. These are family relationships, friendships, romantic relationships, committed relationships, and everlasting relationships. Each of these relationship types will have an impact on you. Each will also impact your partner in different ways.

Before you meet your partner, you will have had family relationships and friendships. With your partner, you may experience a friendship, a romantic relationship, and a committed relationship. What about taking your relationship to the next level—that of an everlasting relationship?

Family Relationships

The relationships that provided you and your partner with the ideas and beliefs you have about love primarily originated from your families. Before you move your relationship with your partner forward, you will need to explore your family relationships.

Family is about having roots. In essence, family is a pure form of connected love. The realm of family is critical and sacred, and it is acknowledged in every person's life, whether by its absence or presence. The existence of family allows for all other relationships to flourish. Broken family relationships can lead to breakdowns and can be detrimental to future relationships. A complete relationship with one's mother and father will encourage generosity, tenderness, and forgiveness. The ancestral history you inherit, the family you're born into, and the circumstances and events that happened to you while you were growing up all have an impact on how you and your partner communicate with and relate to other people.

The gift of declaring yourself complete with your parents will have a lifelong impact on your relationships. This declaration, spoken powerfully to yourself and perhaps to others, will establish a foundation of integrity that allows extraordinary relationships to flourish. You will accept the fact that there is no way your family history could have played out other than the way it did. The experiences you had with your family—both positive and negative—have defined how you were and still are in your other relationships.

Whatever the path of your life to this point, you retain the ultimate creative power over your life. This means you can invent the relationship that reflects who you are. You can have the love you desire. Most people are disconnected from this power.

I often observe what I call "family constellations" with my clients. Their extended families have the same issues as my clients, and the patterns repeat over generations. These patterns may extend back into a family's distant past. We rarely connect these dots, although we do so readily with physical characteristics carried on from generation to generation. Thus it is important to examine your family relationships. You may be able to find the source of issues and conflicts in your own relationships. In fact, one of the first requests I make of my clients who want to improve their relationships with their significant others is that they describe their relationships with their mothers and fathers.

Essentially, we learn how to relate to the people we love through our early experiences with our parents and through the way they related to each other and to us. If a person has a conflicted relationship with her or his parents, it's likely that her or his adult relationships will be conflicted too. The importance of family relationships, both in childhood and adulthood, may surprise you. Many people don't think (or don't want to think) that their relationships with their parents have anything to do with their committed relationships. However, these relationships can be mirror images. The power of parental influence can easily be considered a *blind spot*; an inability to see any connection to their existing or future relationships.

If we have had mostly positive experiences with our parents and they have been loving, respectful, and forgiving, it is likely we possess the innate skills required to create and maintain loving relationships as adults. However, if our early experiences were the opposite of that, it is unlikely we will be able to create and maintain loving relationships because we do not possess the skills.

My clients work at becoming complete with their parents. You need to take this step also in order to experience a natural affinity for your parents. The freedom this creates opens the door to an open, communicative, and loving relationship with those important in your life, from family and friends to your partner.

It may seem like creating loving relationships in your life is hopeless if there are significant familial conflicts that you must first resolve. It can be true that we inherit and unconsciously replicate all kinds of situations (accidents and tragedies, as well as triumphs and generosities) from our ancestral lineage. However, it may also be true that the brilliant aspect of the Self is forever alive and shining, always yearning to be revealed.

The energy of the Self reveals itself in art, music, dance, poetry, and philosophy, as well as in other modes of creativity. This aspect of the Self, which exists within all of us, has the power to transcend history and transform one's inherited family constellation, creating an emerging paradigm of magnificent, loving, and productive relationships. These relationships can be dedicated to impacting the health, peace, and love in all of us for existing and future generations.

Though you'll be tapping into your Self in many different ways while reading this book, the first step toward having a healthy and happy relationship with your parents is to be complete with them. It does not matter whether they are alive or deceased; you need to not harbor any discontent, lingering anger, issues, trauma, or tragedies relative to them. It's essential for any couple that wants to create an extraordinary relationship to be in happy and healthy relationships with their parents. I have noticed that clients who have had, or who presently enjoy, good relationships with their parents have a distinct advantage in creating happy and loving relationships for themselves.

Personally, I have an amazing, loving relationship with my mother and father, though that wasn't always the case. While I was growing up, my father was hard on me. He got angry when I disobeyed my mother. It was me against them. I felt frightened, alone, and confused. My personal breakthrough happened as an adult during a personal development seminar. It hit me like a lightning rod: my father's reactions to my behavior were misguided expressions of his love and commitment. I approached my father. I told him that I knew that he loved me, even though he had never said those words. He was silent. Then he said, "Marty, I love you." For the rest of his life, he consistently spoke of his love for me. He referred to me as his hero. This change in our relationship was one of the most powerful transformations of my life.

Being complete with my parents, though they have both passed on, is a constant source of fulfillment for me. The experience of parental love that is always present for me allows me to continue creating extraordinary relationships. In fact, when I am challenged with difficult situations, just thinking about my parents helps me to transcend potential upsets. Family love is the quintessential foundation for successful relationships.

It may take time, patience, and effort, but when you are able to acknowledge affinity for your family and their role in your happiness and success, all kinds of possibilities and miracles become available to you. An individual who enthusiastically acknowledges her or his parents and family is usually stable, happy, and appreciative of life.

These people tend to be grateful and productive, to contribute to their community, and to participate in loving relationships.

Friendships

We don't choose our parents, but we do choose our friends. This is why friendship holds the potential for extraordinary power. Whether a friendship is long lasting or temporary, there is a kinship there. Usually there is a familial aspect to friendship that allows us to align with one another while receiving an outsider's perspective on our lives. Friends are often compatible in their beliefs, values, and standards but are not necessarily the same kinds of people. Their differences result in more profound relationships.

Friendships provide necessary social support and reinforcement when we are upset, confused, or encountering conflicting options. With a friend, you can get out your thoughts and feelings, allowing issues and problems to become clear. You may not be able to do this by yourself. Friendships can be both nurturing and challenging, enabling you to confront what is relevant in your daily life as well as your blind spots in other relationships.

You may feel fearful about or resistant to communicating an incident to your partner, or you may be experiencing a lack of communication with her or him. In such instances, a good friend can provide a valuable outlet, allowing you to release your fears. You may be able to identify negative impulses you are wrestling with in your own head and bounce them off someone who cares about you. This simple gesture can provide immediate relief and make it easier for you to express yourself to your partner.

Since we select our friends, these relationships are easier to maintain than familial relationships. The attachment in friendship is not the same as it is in romantic relationships. There are friendships that last for long periods of time as well as ones that lose their significance and fall away. The importance of brief friendships should not be overlooked. They can be critical at the time because there is no forced attachment, and they provided you with an essential perspective you could not receive elsewhere.

Sometimes romantic relationships start as friendships.

Romantic Relationships

I regard the romantic stage of a relationship as an illness or a disease. Why? Because the messages being sent throughout your physical body are different than at other times, and your expectations are out of whack. You do not think clearly, you're distracted by your physical and emotional self, and you behave strangely. Unfortunately, romances are often as common and fleeting as the common cold.

In our culture, the romantic phase of a relationship may not actually *be* a relationship, nor does it guarantee any future relationship. In fact, romance is often a momentary, transitory, primarily physical and emotional experience that cannot be counted on to persevere, or to replicate itself, in the future. Romance is just romance; it is not necessarily the prelude to something else.

Though many people choose to get married while in the romantic stage of a relationship, it's important to note that romances do not necessarily lead to committed or everlasting relationships. Most, in fact, do not, hence the high divorce rate.

Though it is possible that couples in romantic relationships can establish an everlasting relationship, there is certainly no causality between the two. You do not have to go through a romantic relationship in order to have an everlasting relationship. One may go through a romantic relationship prior to establishing an everlasting relationship, but it is not necessary for a couple to experience romance before they enter the stage of an everlasting relationship. This is probably the most common misconception about love. Arranged marriages, for example, exhibit success that is not based on the feeling of romantic love, but on the growth of devoted love over time within the marriage.[5]

Romantic relationships can best be characterized by the expression "youandme"—that is, as a unit with no space between the two. When the space for individuality disappears, things can go awry. "Youandme" can turn into something volatile when the only uniqueness you have is your identity as a couple. When you cram two individuals into one entity, love is lost.

Romantic relationships are powerful and can be dangerous; they can have far reaching consequences, which may dramatically and radically influence people's lives. Unfortunately, we have been born into a culture that promotes and fosters the disease called romance. Too often we must pay for buying into this perspective. During the romantic phase, thoughts are often expressed without any intention to follow through. This is disappointing, and often hurtful.

For instance, my clients Larry and Jane fell madly in love. Larry constantly spoke of his lifelong commitment to Jane. Even though the couple hadn't formally committed to one another yet, Jane believed Larry; she started planning their future together. However, while Larry was sincere at the time of his declaration, his words no longer existed in the same way for him once that singular moment of romance had passed. This is because men may experience their words in the moment but do not necessarily have the long-standing vision to uphold those statements into the future. On the other hand, women tend to accept their lover's statements as declarations of love, envisioning men's words to be true both in the moment and well into the future.

Larry was not as devoted as he had originally stated. Jane was devastated. Over time, she became resentful, turning what was once beautiful and romantic into something ugly. The romance ended badly. This kind of quick hookup and equally quick dissolution is common during the romantic stage.

---

[5] Arranged Marriages http://iml.jou.ufl.edu/projects/spring07/zuffoletti/love.html

Women and men who fall in love and experience the romantic stage of a relationship may develop a deep attachment to, or a need for, the other person. This can evolve to the point where one or both people feel unable to be separated from the other. The need is overwhelming and obsessive. This often results in a painful breakup when one partner decides to end the relationship.

Women tend to fall into the trap of romance more often than men do. I assert that this is because more women feel the need to experience a committed relationship. Some want a relationship so much that they skip developing a friendship with their partners, jumping immediately into the romantic phase. This can damage the relationship from the outset because the connection with the partner is based on transitory physical energies. The relationship would ideally be based on the respect and affection of friendship, which tends to be longer lasting.

Committed Relationships

A committed relationship is usually between two individuals. This relationship may or may not be exclusive, based on the agreement of the couple. A polyamorous relationship may also be committed yet include other partners. This kind of committed relationship too may or may not be exclusive. A committed relationship is defined as one that is trusting and that is intended to evolve over time. This does not necessarily mean that the relationship will include marriage or serve as a lifetime commitment.

Everlasting Relationships

The everlasting relationship is distinguished by a powerfully aligned declaration. This relationship will last over a lifetime and assimilates commitment in its highest form. It is a lifelong partnership. The relationship may or may not include marriage. The bonding of the couple is idealistic and transcends differences. Everlasting relationships are rare.

Couples in committed relationships can only aspire to everlasting relationships. Committed relationships are vulnerable to separation. Within an everlasting relationship, however, there is no option. Each partner, day by day and moment by moment, chooses to create the relationship newly. Their vows are a covenant to themselves and to each other, and both partners honor their word as to who they are in their commitment to the lifelong relationship.

The Stages of Exclusive Relationships

The four stages that exclusive relationships can go through are

- *Friendship*, or creating a bond with your partner through honest communication;
- *Romance*, otherwise known as "falling in love," or experiencing a visceral, physical, and emotional attraction to one another;
- *Commitment*, which may include choosing to live together, getting engaged, marrying, and having children; and finally
- *Everlasting relationship*, a magical realm of unconditional love, caring, dedication, and trust that transcends differences.

Exclusive relationships can reach any of these stages, but they may also stall within any of these stages, stopping at a specific stage and failing to progress further. For instance, if you were to fall in love but your partner didn't want to commit, the relationship would have romance and maybe friendship but not commitment (and not everlasting). If you are divorced, then your relationship went through commitment (and maybe friendship and romance), but never reached everlasting. If you or someone you know has been married for decades, the relationship may have progressed through all of the stages and may be an everlasting relationship.

Immersing yourself in the friendship stage is a great foundation for romance and a committed relationship. The friendship stage doesn't contain as much risk as the romantic or committed stages. Plus it offers opportunities, over and over again, to gain knowledge about your partner and yourself as well. If your relationship is based on integrity and authentic communication and you both are complete with your parents, the foundation for your future relationship is established.

Friendship creates a powerful bond that is mutually beneficial and satisfying. This bond has the potential to evolve into the romantic phase. In fact, friends who decide to date often experience a more meaningful transition into romance and, later on, into the commitment phase.

Friends to Lovers

Katherine's primary purpose in life was to be a successful lawyer. Dating and being with men were low on her priority list. Yet there was pressure on her from family and friends. Her mother and father were concerned.

Katherine had little experience in being in a relationship. She signed up with online dating sites to no avail. Then her mother requested she meet a friend's son. Gary was also a lawyer, and the two began seeing each other. Mainly they talked about their careers. Katherine and Gary connected through their mutual appreciation of the world of law, but they were not dating each other. At some point, they began to share their experiences and support each other through the challenges each faced with dating.

During our coaching sessions, Katherine decided there was nothing wrong with her if she was not in a committed relationship.

She adopted the perspective that she could share herself with a man without any agenda. She didn't have to be in a loving relationship with "the one." What transpired was a breakthrough. She discovered an appreciation for opening up her heart, sharing, and listening to a man speak from his reality. Her intention was to develop a trusting, loving friendship.

The affinity that Katherine and Gary had for each other began to emerge. They began to experience a different kind of attraction, and they enjoyed being together. They decided to start dating. The experience was exciting. They knew each other in a way that was inspiring for both of them. After two years, they got married. Their marriage served as the beginning of their romantic phase.

Katherine was empowered by her loving relationship, and her law career flourished. The love story with her husband was magical. Her commitment to deeply appreciate the friendship was a powerful experience that allowed her love and future to manifest. Out of that friendship, Katherine and Gary created an everlasting relationship.

Chapter 9:
Falling in Love Is Not Hard,
but Staying in Love Is

The easiest part of a relationship is falling in love. The immediate attraction can be very powerful, and you may feel as if you're not choosing the other person but being pulled in her or his direction. Even being in the same room with one another can be potent, seductive, and emotional. You may feel that you are just along for the ride or you may feel completely out of control.

There's no courage involved in falling in love. The real test comes after the initial rush of romance is over. When you reach that point in your adventure together, your respective differences begin to rise to the surface. Once you're committed to one another, you're not only considering the current circumstances but also a future together. Every day seems to hold new challenges, while you simultaneously fall into a routine with one another. This is when love gets complicated and requires courage to be sustained.

The Difference between Falling in Love and Staying in Love

So you're in love, and your relationship has moved to a more serious place. Perhaps you've decided to live together or get married, or perhaps you have said your vows and are wondering what's next. The romantic relationship was addictive, enticing, and so great! It seemed like the way that you both were in the relationship would be the way you'd be forever.

The single most common misconception about love is that love is forever. Unfortunately, you'll soon find out that this is sadly not the case. Once you and your partner make a commitment, the romance changes. It isn't like it was during the romantic phase. Being in the romantic stage and the committed stage simultaneously is usually not possible. The transition between the romantic stage and the committed stage is challenging. This is when most of the issues arise, and this is when the breakdowns and breakthroughs happen. The important thing to keep in mind is this: the relationship with your partner will change when you commit.

When people expect the romantic phase to continue into the committed phase—the second most common misconception about love—they are usually disappointed. The contrast often results in disillusionment, confusion, and the feeling that there is a lack of possibility in the relationship. The committed stage is when partners begin to settle into what they expect the relationship to be. This is when the insufficiencies and incompletions of each individual begin to surface.

Many couples get engaged during the romantic stage. If a couple is fortunate enough to experience the friendship stage before moving into romance, then they may make the transition into the committed stage more easily. In the romantic phase, the speaking, listening, and language is often fantasized. When marriages end quickly, it is because the fantasy ends. A disillusioned partner may say "I married a stranger." This usually means the couple jumped into commitment without giving sufficient consideration to friendship, and they married in the romantic stage. Though some relationships can survive rushing into the committed stage, most cannot.

There are two reasons for failure. The first is that what you feel in the romantic stage is not necessarily what you will feel once you commit. In many ways, the feeling, the communication, and the intimacy do not show up as powerfully in the committed phase as they do in the romantic phase. If your expectations were that you would remain madly in love but you find yourself falling into a predictable and boring routine, there will be disappointment. If the intimacy falls away, you will feel disillusioned—even though your relationship has advanced into the commitment you originally wanted.

The second reason is that the experience of love is uniquely different in the romantic phase than in the committed phase. The language and the manner of being "in love" is much more subtle when you are committed; it has a kind of depth and richness that transcends the physical. The love and affection your partner offers may not be as hot and steamy as it was in the romantic stage, but it will be more fulfilling.

My clients often focus on the negativity in their relationships, and they can't see the positive impact of the committed stage. Once they realize that the love, respect, and affinity they are experiencing is different in the committed stage, they begin to adjust their expectations. In fact, for many of my clients, the new reality surpasses their original expectations. An essential principle for my clients is the integrity of keeping their word and keeping their promises to each other. The love they experience in the committed relationship has permanency and takes on a life of its own.

It is important to understand that the committed stage changes how women and men communicate about their relationships, especially during conflict. When men speak, they are speaking honestly in the moment. However, what they say might not occur to them as real an hour later, a day later, or years later. This could be a casual statement like "you are the most beautiful woman I know," or it could be something deeper like "for better or for worse, 'til death do us part."

A woman not only experiences and absorbs the meaning of the words she's saying or hearing in the moment but also sees the past and the future as well. When she's in that place, she is bound by those words in her past, present, and future. Oftentimes the future significance of those words is as important, if not more important, than the words themselves.

When the word "commitment" is brought up in a conversation between a woman and a man, they each often have different interpretations. A woman usually hears the word "commitment" as being important in the present, but equally as important is her belief that there will be a commitment in the future. The woman hears those words in terms of her past and future, in addition to the moment of now. The man simply says what he means in the moment. This can explain why wedding vows do not always translate the same way for women and men.

It is obvious why these differences in communication cause conflict in a committed relationship. A woman dedicated to the commitment she made to her partner will feel that way throughout their time together. If there's an argument or an issue or a fight, she will deal with it within the context of the belief that "this is my life partner." A man may think "she is my life partner," but often that statement fades for him and moves into the distant past where it doesn't have as much meaning in the moment as it does for a woman.

A man usually experiences conflict, with acute sensitivity in the moment, as something serious and significant. A woman may feel the conflict deeply, but she may not experience it as a deal breaker in their relationship.

Once you are in the committed stage, the most important part of overcoming a breakdown is each partner's ability to give up being "right." This principle is critical. One or both of you must give up being "right" as soon as possible in order to show that your commitment to the relationship is greater than any given circumstance. Doing this demonstrates courage beyond words, and it will have a significant influence on the quality and longevity of the relationship.

You will need to develop the perspective that *there is more about your partner you do not know than you do know*. This is essential. This perspective will allow you to create and re-create the relationship with your partner into the future.

Chapter 10:
Deal Breakers for Committed Relationships

The first question I ask couples who are creating a committed relationship or planning a marriage is "How will the two of you be with each other and relate to each other when this relationship is over?" There is no guarantee a relationship will last forever, so this is a powerful question for any couple to consider.

The conversation about this question will require a context of trust and respect. It may reveal unspoken aspects of each individual's commitments to the relationship. Ultimately, considering the answers to this question can powerfully support each person in identifying issues that may not have been addressed earlier in the relationship.

There are many reasons why a committed relationship may come to an end. One of the most common reasons for divorce today is "irreconcilable differences." This means that there are multiple explanations for why a couple can no longer be together. However, my own experience with my clients has illustrated for me the underlying reasons that many committed relationships end, and there is one primary reason.

It is vital that the woman in relationship be able to share her vision of the future. If her overall perspective is to be a source of integrity for her partner, this will allow the relationship to flourish. When he is unwilling to accept the future she points to, her power and commitment to the relationship is severely diminished. A relationship will end when the man believes the woman is no longer a contribution to him. If he decides that what she is expressing in her commitment is not acceptable, he is no longer open to her unique perspective. When this occurs, the man is no longer being sourced by the woman, and the relationship devolves into mediocrity. Then the relationship is vulnerable. One or both partners may decide to end the relationship and move on, or worse, they may remain stuck in mediocrity. This is the primary reason that committed relationships end, and it is rarely acknowledged.

Additional deal breakers are directly related to philosophical differences that were not resolved prior to the commitment. These philosophical differences can be the partners' individual relationships to God and spirituality, children and family, money and careers, or lifestyle and future plans. There may be differences between their views on monogamy, financial decisions, sexual preferences, and "cheating." A primary deal breaker is emotional or physical abuse. Being in a relationship with a partner who has an unhealthy way of dealing with problems and breakdowns is also a potential deal breaker.

For a successful relationship to flourish, it is essential for both partners to be able to constructively argue. Both must realize that the argument is trivial compared to their love for and commitment to each other. Feeling one has to win every argument, no matter how significant or trivial, is a deal breaker.

Another deal breaker is if one or both partners has a negative addiction. This can be an addiction to work, alcohol, drugs, gambling, or pornography. Addictions to being right or to suffering, obsessions, and other negative issues can also serve as deal breakers in a committed relationship.

More "Reasons" that Committed Relationships End

- I am no longer in love with you.
- I had no idea what it really takes to be married.

- I can no longer be myself.
- You/we have changed.
- I am happier alone.
- You're better off without me.
- I've outgrown you.

Your commitment to marriage may not last over time. The declaration of commitment often fades as time passes. Failure to recreate that promise in daily life opens up the possibility of a breach or a breakdown. I often see that one or both partners in a committed relationship no longer honor the original declaration. This causes an internal integrity violation that, whether it was committed consciously or not, is unacceptable. This is how two fundamentally good people who are in love can, over time, lose touch with the commitment that originally bound them together, even though they may remain the same individuals who fell in love with each other.

Unfortunately, deal breakers in committed relationships seem to be more the rule than the exception. My client Carla was in her fifties and had never been married. She hired me to help her create a relationship with a great man. Being married was secondary. Carla wanted to be in a loving, harmonious relationship.

Attractive and successful, Carla had plenty of interested men to choose from. She began a relationship with a man she really liked. He seemed to meet all the criteria that she had established in our coaching sessions. Then one day a car cut them off while they were driving. He lost his temper and began screaming at the other driver. His tirade continued all the way home. When Carla tried to speak about what happened, he was unwilling to talk about it or even address his reactions.

In our coaching, Carla pointed out his negative outbursts so that she would be able to support him. However, he was unwilling to discuss any responsibility he bore in the situation. He dismissed her, and therefore she was unable to contribute to him. Although their relationship had been loving and compatible, it was clear this was a relationship Carla needed to complete.

She ended the relationship with dignity, empowered to develop what was next for her. She realized that she needed to be with a man who could have a healthy relationship with arguments and breakdowns. Carla's understanding of herself deepened. She became able to discuss any subject or challenge that confronted her, both within and outside of her relationships with men.

Notes to Myself

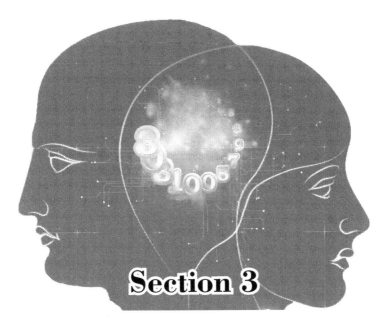

Section 3

Gender Balancing

Chapter 11:
Genderless—Before Women and Men

We are each born with physical sex characteristics. We almost always become attached to that sex, and our self-image may be that of either a woman or a man. Most people go through their lives identifying as only one sex, either female or male. This is a limited perspective. In reality, both feminine and masculine energies exist in every woman and man. You have masculine energies if you are a woman and feminine energies if you are a man.

In working with a diversity of clients, I have been able to see both energies in both sexes—that is, I can see how feminine and masculine characteristics and language clearly contain an integration of both feminine and masculine energies. Most people are unaware of this, and that causes an imbalance, which reduces the power and possibility of owning one's own total Self. With this comes the inability to live as a whole human being. The imbalance causes a gap in the expression of Self as an all-encompassing human being.

However, you *can* distinguish your feminine and masculine energies in a way that frees up the integration. Doing so will allow you to connect to every aspect of your internal feminine and masculine energies. You can create for yourself the perfect balance of 100 percent female and 100 percent male.

Note that individuals with this balance—100 percent female and 100 percent male—allow these composite energies to be a resource for all of humankind. This means such individuals can create relationships beyond our imagination.

Chapter 12:
The Woman and Man Within You

When speaking to groups about relationships, I often begin by asking them, "Did you choose your sex? Did you consciously choose to be a woman or a man?" Many people don't know how to respond to this question. This is because our sex (whether we have female or male anatomy) and our gender identity (whether we see ourselves as feminine or masculine) are often intertwined into a single identity. Numerous sociological, cultural, and familial factors influence our personalities and behavior. How feminine or masculine we seem is largely based on the norms of the culture we live in. Even now, most societies consider sex and gender as one and the same.

I ask my audiences those questions in order to stimulate their thinking about gender identity. Our physical bodies only represent one aspect of who we are as human beings. The other aspects are hidden. However, the hidden aspects of who we are impact our relationships with other people. What is hidden about us can have a particularly significant impact on our intimate relationships, especially once we're past the romance stage and are committed to a partner.

We all have hidden feminine and masculine energies within us that play into our behaviors, personalities, and relationships. Though female energies and male energies can be seen as yin and yang—that is, as opposites—these are in reality two sides of the same coin. And that coin is within each one of us.

Most people have no idea they have both feminine and masculine energies inside them. They are unaware of the ongoing conflict within, so they do not recognize that this is what creates conflict when they attempt to communicate their truths to other people. The key is to balance your energies. This will allow for expanded communication and harmony with your partner and others, transcending gender bias. From a spiritual perspective, there is no sexuality, and therefore there is no gender.

Chapter 13:
Discovering Your Feminine
and Masculine Energies

The first step in learning how to distinguish the woman and man within you is to determine what this really means. Everyone has feminine and masculine energies in her or his personality and way of being. In fact, everything contains different percentages of these energies.

This is most easily seen in animals. If you have a pet, you have probably observed this. Some female dogs and cats have dominant masculine energy, whereas other female pets are passive and feminine. The same can be said for male dogs and cats, as well as for other animals. The interesting thing about using pets as an example is they don't have cultural expectations or societal norms to conform to. Their personalities are innate, and their behaviors are primarily instinctual. Humans, however, are heavily influenced by cultural standards, societal norms, and family expectations—a multitude of energies that shape our personalities. Because of this, our ways of being in the world are less innate, less instinctual, and less in tune with the woman and man that naturally live inside each of us.

For humans, the feminine and masculine energies are often imbalanced because of the pressures to keep our personalities in sync with our sex or perceived gender. These pressures can come from society, from school, and from other cultural institutions, as well as from family, friends, and colleagues.

The inherent conflict that happens as a result of being out of balance can be resolved by distinguishing the woman and man within you. When you achieve this, you will allow all aspects of yourself to be expressed equally. Your physical being, your feminine being, and your masculine being will be communicating with the rest of the world, allowing your inner self to experience peace, calm, and freedom. This will empower you in your relationships.

If everyone were to attain that balance, the world would transform. The vast, static differences we now perceive between how women and men communicate, feel, behave, and generally experience life would disappear. Notions about who a man is "supposed" to be and who a woman is "supposed" to be would no longer influence the culture. We would all be able to combine feminine and masculine energies into one complete human being. The world would be a better, more loving, and peaceful place.

Table of Feminine and Masculine Energies

Female	Male
Spiritual	Physical
Water	Fire
Being	Doing
Nonlinear	Linear
Listening	Speaking
Manager	Generator
Visionary	Realist
Invisible	Visible
Emotional	Logical
Questioning	Certain
Complex	Fundamental
Past/Present/Future	Present/Now
Passive	Aggressive
Respond	React
Compassionate	Passionate
Enchanting	Romantic
Dance	Force
Patient	Anger
Context	Content

As you can see from the examples in the table above, which are subjective, energies identified as male tend to be physical, while energies identified as female are emotional and spiritual. Male energy represents strength, force, building, and certainty, and it is tactile. Female energy is about listening, guiding, helping, sourcing, and communicating. Female energy is being; male energy is doing. Female energy is within the process; male energy is in attaining the result.

There are feminine and masculine energies within everything, even inanimate objects. For example, subjectively speaking, the sunlight coming through the window is female, whereas the chair you sit on is male. With human beings, feminine and masculine energies are attributed most often to personality traits. Empathy is female; structure is male. Exhibiting more male traits is not any better or worse than having more female traits.

If you are a woman, you may note that you are sometimes domineering or angry. Your male traits are indeed there. As a man, you might be nurturing with your children. You may be highly spiritual. Your female energies are indeed there.

Women tend to communicate in nonlinear ways with words like *love, caring, commitment, future,* and *relationship* taking on a depth of meaning. On the other hand, the male tends to communicate in ways that are primarily linear. This means he is physical and visual. Men mainly exist in the present, and they don't necessarily connect a future meaning to their words. A man can communicate like a woman by instinctively revealing his feminine energies. Conversely, a woman can speak in a linear and direct way by utilizing her masculine energies. This requires the awareness that both a woman and a man exist within.

Prior to balancing your female and male energies, you are primarily at the effect of your imbalance. Your actions are overwhelmingly automatic and reactive. This can be changed. The goal is not to have a fifty-fifty division in which your female energies make up one half and the male energies the other half. On the contrary, when your feminine and masculine energies are balanced, you will attain a hundred percent of each.

Distinguishing the Woman and Man Within You

While doing the following exercise, you will need to suspend your attachment to being a woman or being a man. If you are open to the possibility that there is a combination of gender energies within you that, once distinguished and realized, can alter your life and your relationships, then you are ready to get started.

Using the Table of Feminine and Masculine Energies on page 65, cover up the "female" and "male" headers for each of the columns. Then review the list of attributes and pick the words that seem to drive you, describe you, or represent you most clearly. Write down at least four. Remember, this is subjective, and there is no right or wrong combination of energies. When you are finished, review your list. You may have picked four, five, six, or even eight words.

Next, whittle that list down to four predominant energies that best describe you. When eliminating words, think about this: everything you wrote down lives within you. All of those descriptive words are correct, but there are four words that stand out as the most accurate descriptions of you as a person. Once you have that list of four words, look at the table again. This time, uncover the headers.

Add up the number of energies you ascribed to yourself that are male, and repeat the process for the female energies. Then score yourself this way: each energy contributes 25 percent of a possible 100 percent for each gender. In other words, the range is from 100/0 female/male to 0/100 female/male. For example, if you chose *physical* (male), *manager* (female), *doing* (male), and *past/present/future* (female) as your four words, your score would be 50/50 female/male. If you chose *visionary* (female), *spiritual* (female), *doing* (male), and *past/ present/future* (female), your score would be 75/25 female/male.

What's your score? Are you 50/50 female/male? Or 25/75 female/male? Or 100/0 female/male? Whatever your percentages may be, they are a starting point and are malleable. Your balance will shift as you begin to distinguish your feminine and masculine energies.

Feel free to return to this exercise to take an inventory of your changing energy percentages. Note that you are moving forward. You will begin to see your imbalances dramatically shift. This exercise is one of many different ways to distinguish and observe how your feminine and masculine energies manifest themselves in your thoughts, actions, and behaviors.

I once did this exercise with a corporate leadership trainer. This dynamic woman had achieved a high level of success in her field. Before doing the exercise, I asked her to guess what her energy percentages would be. She guessed 75 percent female and 25 percent male, but her result was 100 percent male and 0 percent female. When I revealed the results, she was shocked. I told her that, in my professional opinion, she appeared to be 95 percent male and 5 percent female. She was still shocked. This revelation caused a breakthrough in my client's life. My perspective opened her up to the possibility that a pattern of relying on her male energies for business purposes was impacting the rest of her life. She realized her imbalances were getting in the way of her personal goals.

As a result of our work together, my client learned how to distinguish her feminine and masculine energies. She then successfully shifted, softening her response and gradually balancing the dominant male energy with her emerging female energy. Soon after this, she met and married the man of her dreams. These are the kind of results that are available to you too. If you make a commitment to balancing your feminine and masculine energies, your life will change.

Chapter 14:
The Impact of Gender Imbalance

Mildred and James were heading for a messy divorce. Mildred didn't trust James to follow through on any aspect of their marriage, from everyday household chores to bigger tasks, like disciplining the children and managing their money. This was causing many problems because they were raising two teenagers and working as partners in a business together.

As their coach, I could see that Mildred was letting her male energy take over in a dominant way. She wanted control over the doing and took charge of all the masculine roles in the relationship. No matter how loving, how thoughtful, how kind, how protective, how reliable, how responsible, or how committed James proved himself to be, it was never enough for Mildred. None of his efforts made a difference. This shattered his self-confidence. There didn't seem to be any room in their relationship for his energies or his contribution.

I explained to them how this sort of imbalance didn't happen overnight. Instead, it happened gradually. For example: let's say one day, James takes out the trash. He doesn't realize the bag is broken and leaves garbage scattered from the kitchen all the way outside. Mildred might mention this to him without criticism the first time, but the second or third time, she gives up. Pretty soon, James is not "allowed" to take out the trash because Mildred's male energies have stepped in to take care of the task, to take care of the doing. When

I used this example with Mildred and James, they were surprised. Neither had thought about their dynamic in this manner. It was only at this point, when both of them could acknowledge the imbalance in the expression of their respective energies, that a marked shift was able to take place.

Mildred decided to ease back on her tendency to allow her male energies to take over so that James could take on more responsibilities. In return, James began to handle more of the family's "doing" tasks, and he was excited about having more responsibilities. Once James was handling more of the male aspects of the relationship, Mildred was able to tap into her female energies, because she didn't feel the need to dominate every situation.

Mildred and James had allowed an imbalance to happen. This occurred when Mildred took over James's established role of doing. Though their story depicts traditional gender roles, it could have just as easily happened the opposite way, with James taking over all the feminine roles within their relationship.

Note that balancing their energies didn't require a change in their personalities or who Mildred and James were as people. They made a conscious choice to return to the way they were with each other before their energies shifted out of balance. The shift in perspective allowed them to behave more naturally, not only with each other but also in the rest of their lives.

What I've discovered is that an imbalance of feminine and masculine energies often stems from shifting roles within a couple. When you begin a relationship and handle day-to-day tasks like James and Mildred did, any switch in how you both handle the tasks can cause an imbalance over time. Sometimes the imbalance starts with something small like the hole in the trash bag. Sometimes it's caused by a more significant event, conflict, or difference. No matter what the cause, it is essential to be balanced, and once you are conscious of this, the shift is not difficult.

Balancing Energies

In a perfect world, everyone would have perfectly balanced feminine and masculine energies. We would all live as complete human beings. However, consider that the world is perfect, including all its imperfections, and so are human beings. Fortunately, it's relatively easy to work toward a total balance once you become aware that there is, in fact, an imbalance and once you are committed to distinguishing that imbalance within you.

Being 100/100 is unlike being 50/50. The latter implies a division of power, while in reality, using all of your feminine and masculine energies is about attaining that balance in order to be personally empowered. With 100/100, all your energies are available to you. For women, this means it is essential to embrace the fundamental, innate feminine energies of the woman within while simultaneously assimilating those male energies that make up the man within. For men, this means being able to include the female energies that are within and aligning them with the masculine energies that are already present.

Regardless of whether you're a woman or a man, it may feel more natural to you to behave and communicate in a feminine or masculine way. If you are ambidextrous, you can use both hands. With a 100/100 balance of energies, you can use both energies with equal skill and equal results.

When you are at 50/50, half of your energies—half of your female energies and half of your male energies—aren't being expressed. You're essentially deleting or leaving out half of what's available within you. In contrast, 100/100 includes everything. This is an inclusive representation of the essence of who you really are in the fullest sense of being human. There's no longer a distinction between feminine and masculine; everything blends together into who you are, what your full potential is, and how you are expressing that in your life at every moment.

Using the Table of Feminine and Masculine Energies, you already began to distinguish the feminine and masculine energies within. Even if you struggled with your own assessment, you are now starting to become conscious that you have both types of energies inside and that both are exhibited in your behaviors and your personality. If you suspect that your energies are in conflict or that one gender might be overpowering another, you should realize that this is completely normal.

A good way to identify your energies and the balance within is to observe how you react to situations and in communicating with other people. How do you respond to stressful or trying circumstances? If something upsets you, observing your reaction can provide you with an opportunity to assess how much feminine and masculine energies are at play. For instance, if your partner said something argumentative, passive aggressive, or upsetting, how would you react? Are you quick to anger? Does the conflict escalate into yelling and name-calling? Do you instantly go from happy to furious? Does your anger accelerate quickly, from zero to sixty? Are you ready to have an argument the moment your partner opens her or his mouth?

The imbalance can show up in any relationship or situation with another person. It can occur with a friend who rubs you the wrong way, a boss or mentor who wants to share some tough-to-hear criticism, or even a parent whose concern has become overbearing or irritating. You can observe the imbalance in your own thoughts when you argue with, or invalidate yourself.

Regardless of what or who you are reacting to, if you find that you're angry, you are using male energy. However, if you react by not reacting—by removing yourself from the situation, being empathetic, or by otherwise creating a context for the conflict, your female energy is being manifested.

By taking a conscious step back on a day-to-day basis to observe what your instinctive reactions are to a variety of situations, you may provide an opening for the opposing energy to become present.

For example, if you find that you tend to react in a predominantly male way by being critical, negative, or angry in response to stress, observe this, and then allow your female energy to become present. In fact, the observation itself will create some space for you to allow your female energy to emerge. Instead of reacting with anger, you can allow yourself to hear what the other person is saying. On the flip side, if you are predominantly female in your response to stress and conflict, observing your response might support you in asserting yourself. You may then be able to express how you are feeling or what your side of the issue is.

Making the conscious effort to observe your energies and to be balanced will improve your communication skills. This will be true with your partner as well as with friends, family members, coworkers, and others in your life.

An important step in balancing your energies and getting to 100/100 is to realize that your reactions are tied to female or male energies. When you're in a stressful situation, if you consistently react by thinking *I'm going to do this* or *I should do this* or *I need to fix this*, then you are utilizing the male energies. These are the energies that tell you to handle the situation and fix the problem. However, if you stop to notice what role your female energies are playing in that moment, the reaction will seem passive in comparison.

Try to pay more attention to how you are behaving throughout your day. Don't attempt to change how you are behaving; simply observe yourself. The observation process is subjective. You are the judge and jury of your own responses, reactions, and emotions. What you perceive as the energy you are displaying is your opinion, and there's nothing right or wrong about that. You're just labeling your experience as you see it. The observation itself allows an opening for the opposing energy to present itself or to come into perspective.

Observe where you're using male energies. Most people use their male energies while at work for problem solving and tasks that require a lot of "doing." Observe where you are using female energies. This may be when you are with children or when you are listening to a friend, colleague, or family member discuss an issue about a relationship. The most important part of this step is the observation. The more you actively observe how you are behaving in different situations, the more naturally your respective energies will be revealed.

If you find you rely on predominantly male energies, just notice that. You may think, *Hmm, I see I'm being predominantly male throughout my day.* That's enough; there's no need, at this point, to change your behavior.

As you continue to focus on observing your behaviors, you will naturally integrate the opposite energy. This will happen over time because you are committed to the balancing act that becoming 100/100 requires. The more you distinguish among feminine and masculine energies, the more the natural order will occur. Soon this will become how you respond and relate to everyday life and the people in it, including your partner.

Chapter 15:
An Ideal Balance of Feminine and Masculine Energies

Every man has his woman within him and every woman has her man within her. Only the meditator comes to know his whole being. Suddenly his inner woman and the inner man melt and merge into each other. That creates an orgasmic state in him. Now it is no more a momentary experience that comes and goes; it is something that continues, day in and day out, like the heart beating or breathing.

—Osho[6]

When the feminine and masculine energies are in balance, there will be a consistent experience of being at peace. When you are in balance, you will have an affinity for the people in your life. Your response at any given moment, in any kind of situation or circumstance, will be appropriate and will represent you. How you respond will resonate, communicating the essence of who you are. You will be empowered by how you represent yourself while being able to deeply understand others. You will be able to hear what they are saying without assigning value or judgment. You will be able to re-create others' viewpoints without agreeing or disagreeing.

[6] Osho, http://www.shift.is/2013/10/20-transformational-truths-from-sages-through out-the-ages/

You will have come to a place where you respect yourself without reacting and taking what others say personally. Instead, you will have an innermost attitude of accepting others' behaviors, words, and opinions as their own truths. That way, you can be empathetic toward who you are listening to, regardless of your evaluations. This means that there will be no second-guessing and no questioning that other people are listening to you completely. It will be as if the tone and the intention of your speaking and listening is that of being whole and complete. The experience is one of being authentic and transparent.

When you reach a balance of 100/100, this will not be the end. In fact, balance is a state of being that you will continue to strive toward by consistently observing your feminine and masculine energies until it becomes natural. Realizing the total balance of all your energies is an ultimate state of being, one which you can aspire to fulfill throughout your lifetime. Observing your feminine and masculine energies is the first step in working toward a total balance. The second step is becoming responsible for both your feminine and masculine energies. The third step is acting consistently with all your energies, finally ready to generate your Self as a complete human being.

Women today tend to rely on their male energies. This has an effect on their relationships because an individual's predominant energy will influence who they will attract and who they will turn off. In my experience as a coach, I've noticed that when women who have strong male energies gravitate toward men with equally predominant male energies, the result is a high-octane, high-conflict relationship that usually ends in a fiasco. But when they gravitate toward men with a significant amount of female energy, the result is less combustible. Women seek balance in a partner, so they tend to be attracted to men who have the qualities they themselves lack. The primary problem with this kind of relationship is that you can't reach your own inner balance by seeking it from someone else.

When a woman who has predominantly male energies dates a

man with significant amounts of female energy, the results are not satisfying. Even though the woman is seeking his female energy as a balance for her own male energies, the man may eventually seem weak or less than "manly" enough to support her. This causes conflict in the relationship. However, if the woman were to observe her own energies and tap into her female energy when appropriate, this would allow a man with significant female energies to manifest his own male energies within their relationship. The energies would align, allowing for an equitable balance.

My clients Susan and Greg provide the perfect example. Susan had primarily male energy and was comfortable around men. From my experience working with high-powered women, I suspected that Susan had a female side she wasn't as comfortable expressing. Her husband Greg had a strong, but not necessarily predominant, female energy. He had a remarkable balance of feminine and masculine energy. Susan was attracted to Greg because of his female energies but also because his male energies allowed her to feel safe enough to express her female energies.

Greg and Susan's relationship was solid. However, Susan wanted coaching that would help them transform their relationship to have it be extraordinary. I was happy to help. We needed to focus on balancing Susan's energies. With her commitment to that—and Greg's positive responses and encouragement—they learned how to maintain a 100/100 balance together. This is one of the fundamental building blocks for an everlasting relationship.

For most women who express predominantly male energy, achieving balance and being at 100/100 requires letting go of what they are *doing* in their everyday life to generate a focus on who they are *being*. What this usually translates to is transcending the need to control.

The story I shared about Mildred and James provides a great example of how women with predominantly male energies may exert too much control over the relationship. Over time, Mildred took control over everything, including the tasks that had been James's responsibilities. When Mildred balanced her male energy with her female energy by letting go of her control over all the responsibilities in the relationship, her life changed. Whatever responsibilities were hers at the beginning of their relationship remained Mildred's. But she did relinquish some responsibilities back to James. This allowed Mildred to take more of a managerial role, which uses female energies.

If you are a woman who is using predominantly male energies in your life and your relationship, it is important to allow your female energies to surface and replace the male energies. Remember, female energies don't feel the same as male energies, so you won't feel like you're *doing* anything in the process; this is because female energy primarily requires you to just *be*.

For a lot of women, the prospect of trying this process is scary, but the world won't fall apart when you stop controlling it. In fact, when you do ease up on the reins and allow someone else to be responsible for certain tasks in your relationship and your family, this will allow you to tap into what you're truly good at: being a manager and a visionary. Instead of spending your time controlling and doing, you'll have time to take on the perspective that you have as the woman in the relationship—simultaneously seeing the past, present, and future.

When women and men become aligned with the woman and man within themselves and are able to use their feminine and masculine energies in equal measure (in other words, at 100/100), there is a breakthrough in their relationships.

Nathan was a successful entrepreneur who predominantly used his female energy. He was married to a woman with predominant male energy. His approach to life was soft, caring, and empathetic. He avoided arguments, yelling, and confrontation. In our coaching, Nathan realized that he had resistance to taking a position that might upset anyone else. He saw that he could not gain his masculine energies from his wife. He observed that he was being used by his feminine energy in a way that did not support him or his relationship. He was able to see how fear and resistance to being upset limited his power.

Nathan's passions began to surface. He trusted his experience to communicate when something was bothering him so that what was being revealed was truthful. He began to feel comfortable taking positions and expressing how he felt. He was being proactive, rather than reactive, inside his male energy. This allowed his internal balance of feminine and masculine energies to evolve. Nathan began to trust in his experience as a powerful leader. This impacted his relationship with his wife, who began to observe and balance her own energies. Now Nathan and his wife are actively engaged in creating an everlasting relationship.

The Impact of Being Totally Balanced

The amazing thing about balancing feminine and masculine energies is that there is a significant impact on a relationship even if only one partner is conscious of the woman and man within. When one partner is committed to being in balance, the results are immediate in the number and kind of disagreements they will have together.

If you seek balance, the cascade of reactions to your differences will diminish. This is because you will allow your reactions to be tempered so that they are less automatic. When your energies are balanced, you will accept that your partner's opinion or perspective is just that—an opinion or a perspective. It is not in opposition to you personally or to what you have together as a couple. In other words, what your partner says will no longer feel like a threat or a problem; it just exists. It is what it is. There can be differences without arguments because you'll be able to discuss those differences in a rational manner. If you respect your partner's opinions and perspectives, she or he will respect yours.

Try this for yourself. You should discover that the reaction and the change in dynamic are instantaneous. When you are living with the dynamic of being totally balanced, the potential for conflict is minimized, even obliterated, by the fact that it's impossible to have a one-sided fight. When you're committed to being balanced and to having your relationship evolve, you are responsible for yourself. There may not be anything your partner needs to do or change. By changing *your* actions and shifting *your* way of being, you will transform the dynamic of your relationship. In this way, one person can make an enormous contribution to transforming the relationship from mediocre to extraordinary.

In my own life, I went from using predominantly male energy in my relationships with women to creating greater female energy. This affected the balance within my relationship with my wife. When I'm predominantly using my male energies, she instinctively responds by utilizing her female energies; however, when I'm using my female energies, she naturally and instinctively shifts to her male energies, causing a harmonious balance. She observes the shifts in our dynamic, and I am simultaneously aware of her response to my always-changing energies.

After being married for more than thirty years, our conversations have become a beautiful dance. This dance allows for the balance of our respective energies, providing us with a natural and easy way of relating to each other. We accept conflicts because we relate naturally at both the silliest and the deepest levels. Our gender differences have significantly dissolved. This is a prime example of how energies can interchange between two people in an authentic way. All that is required is that one partner be focused and intentional about the gender energies being expressed. If both partners are focused and intentional, this creates even greater power.

When you are striving for total balance, what could be adversarial or oppositional will be diffused. Because you have learned to appreciate everything about your partner, you can embrace the differences without worrying about the consequences for your relationship. If one person in a couple is consciously balancing her or his feminine and masculine energies, this will move the relationship closer to "you and me." Balancing your energies teaches you how to be empathetic, understanding, and communicative with your partner in a respectful way, allowing both individuals to be heard. You are able to discover who you are and who your partner is by being with her or him in an open, accepting way, free of judgment, blame, or conflict.

When you are balanced with all your feminine and masculine energies, a difference of opinion isn't a make-it-or-break-it fight; it's an opportunity to learn about each other as individuals and to learn about yourselves as a couple. The closer you get to being conscious of and able to distinguish among your own feminine and masculine energies, the easier it will be to identify your partner's feminine and masculine energies and to achieve your ultimate balance.

When you balance your own inner energies and are able to tap into the woman and man within, you are no longer at war with yourself. There is no struggle for or against dominance. You create a sense of peace, which opens the door to creating the extraordinary relationship you have long dreamed of having.

Learning to distinguish the woman and man within is one of my most powerful and popular seminar topics. This is the heart of my coaching with my clients. The act of balancing and acknowledging the woman and man within has transformed thousands of people's lives and relationships. Working toward a balance of my own feminine and masculine energies has empowered my marriage. You can do the same in your own relationships, creating a balanced partnership and committed relationship that is built to last.

Notes to Myself

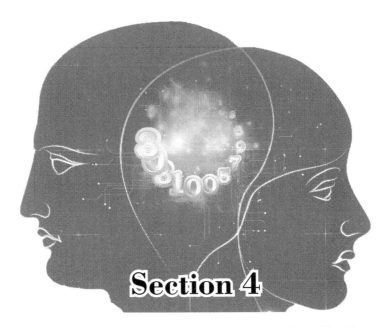

Section 4

An Evolutionary Model

Chapter 16:
Communication: Your Pathway to Love

The most common answer to the question "What does it take to be in a successful relationship?" is communication. Yet what is meant by *communication* is not fully understood. Most people are fundamentally unaware that their conversations are taking place in many different realms at once. These realms include those of being right, being social, being interesting, trying to look good, attempting to impart information, sharing ideas, and taking actions. Some people have no purpose for communicating other than talking. Rarely does someone preface her or his communication in order to create a context for what it is intended for.

However, consider that powerful communication begins with the listener rather than the speaker. The effective communicator is clear that speaking emanates from the power of listening. Therefore, the listening is what primarily generates the speaking and thus impacts and influences the entire communication. For this reason, when one communicates with the intention of creating love and intimacy, the possibility of a magical union becomes clear.

When you speak, your communication works *simultaneously* on the following three levels:

- The words you speak
- The commitment that is driving those words (often hidden)
- That which is not spoken but which is present and rarely acknowledged (internal conversations)

These three levels can create an entangled perspective. The listener may not hear what the speaker means to say. In this way, the listener is not realizing the intention of what was spoken.

In this form of communicating, the unspoken has the greatest influence and impact on the conversation. This is not the intention of either the speaker or the listener. Ideally, you are striving to have one voice, so that the words you speak are generated by the clarity of your commitment. Your internal conversations are nothing more than conversations. When not communicated, what you say to yourself gives power to those conversations. In fact, they may appear to you to be the truth.

In addition to not communicating your internal conversations, you may be gathering evidence to substantiate the truth about those unspoken conversations. Those conversations will devolve into a reality that severely limits your expression of love. If you do not communicate those background conversations, it will have a negative impact on your relationships. When communicated responsibly, however, the significance will be diffused, enlightening the conversation.

Expressing yourself through communication at all levels, holding nothing back, allows intimacy to reveal itself. This means it is important to express what you are most concerned or frightened by. The phenomenon of powerfully and authentically communicating inside your loving relationship causes love and intimacy to be present. This kind of full communication also provides you with a newfound freedom to express yourself with one voice throughout your life.

The act of communicating an experience of love allows for a wide range of expression, covering all aspects of truth, imagination, fantasy, poetry, and art. The unspoken magic of expressing love from one to another is inspiring, creating a realm of possibility that goes beyond our existing reality and causing a profound shift in our relations to one another and to life.

Listening for Love

It is essential to generate the courage to suspend all of your negative conversations about what is happening. This means having a willingness to sacrifice all you believe for the sake of entering into another's world. This means literally and arbitrarily giving up all your rights to redirect your life and way of being into another person's reality and transcending your identity in the process. You are now listening from a space of nothing. Within that space of nothing, everything and anything becomes possible. Your personal experience of listening to and connecting with another person is the greatest gift you can give yourself and others.

Consider that love expressed is often perceived as unrequited love. Yet the key is to listen for love in any and all forms and to know that a smile, a look, a touch, or a word may in fact communicate an infinite expression of love.

Chapter 17:
Declaring Your Primary Commitments

We live in a world where feelings, moods, and circumstances shape the lives and futures of human beings. Fortunately, there has been a breakthrough in the way in which people live. There is a growing community of committed individuals who are causing a transformation by shifting away from being at the mercy of their feelings and circumstances and instead shifting toward generating decisions and life choices based on their primary commitments. The old way of being limits individuals' futuristic abilities to evolve.

Within the existing paradigm, our feelings and circumstances have been the governing forces in living life as we know it. The emerging paradigm reveals a new set of primary commitments. These commitments are designed to create a context for our actions, and they supersede any and all feelings and circumstances. This does not mean we do not acknowledge and express our feelings; it does mean that our feelings are no longer running the show and determining the direction of our futures.

Examples of Primary Commitments

The following are examples of primary commitments:

- Maintaining your well-being and overall wellness
- Communicating freely and responsibly with no limitations

- Loving and being loved
- Loving the career of your choice
- Having financial freedom
- Having a relationship to spirituality
- Making a difference in people's lives
- Creating a future that empowers you and your family
- Living as if the best years of your life are ahead of you
- Being in an extraordinary relationship
- Loving life and having fun
- Empowering others
- Having a purpose that serves humanity

The above are some examples of primary commitments, and not necessarily what you are committed to. By developing and including your primary commitments, you will accelerate and empower all aspects of your life to go beyond anything you could have dreamed or imagined. The emergence of a world generated by primary commitments is the basis of the new paradigm. This is the paradigm that will make possible a world that works for everyone.

Chapter 18:
Creating a Power-Source Relationship

Nothing is more powerful than an idea whose time has come.

—Victor Hugo[7]

The power and possibility of a "sourceful" relationship is limitless. What I mean by sourceful is each partner being 100 percent responsible for the success or failure of the relationship. This relationship transcends the old model of relationship as a 50/50 commitment. It allows for their partnership to be one of two leaders merging as one. A sourceful relationship is created by an extraordinarily dynamic couple. Such a couple transcends circumstances and situations, including the cultures that may have limited this model of relationship.

This type of relationship is rare and requires an unconditional surrender and trust of both individuals. Without this sourceful relationship, it is impossible for extraordinary couples to breakthrough into the forefront. There are few models of this "power-source relationship" in existence.

We have yet to understand the infinite possibilities that this new model of relationship will create into the future. This breakthrough relationship is untapped, under wraps, and yearning to emerge. It represents an idealistic relationship among women and men that

---

[7] Victor Hugo quote, http://www.brainyquote.com/quotes/quotes/v/victorhugo 136258.html

creates unlimited power and possibility. This is all created from the future, and it empowers relationships in present time.

A universal stand for the commitment to empower women is critical to accelerating the power-source relationship in couples. It is essential for women to experience an aligned and collective power and energy. This allows women and men to experience power and to experience being known beyond our existing culture. Women and men standing together for women, creating a universal alignment, is crucial for transcending the condition of patriarchy.

Fortunately, there is now an opening for this model of a power-source relationship to be revealed. Metaphorically, the woman is more often the primary source within a relationship. This is because most women have an innate relationship with fundamental integrity. A woman's relationship to the truth in the physical universe is closer to the actual truth than a man's. Combining this power with her natural visionary ability allows a woman to stand as a resource without limitation.

The man in the power-source relationship is exceptional in his courage and unyielding commitment to empower (trust) the woman to be the source in the relationship. This man is uniquely powerful in consciously knowing himself and building his future to be aligned with empowering the woman. His role is to consistently feed his power to the woman. He supplies electricity to her battery. In turn, she replenishes all his power above and beyond the power she receives.

This dynamic relationship is highly contagious. Being around and observing this kind of power-source relationship will positively impact other people in this couple's world. The two individuals in such a relationship are inspiring, profoundly generous, deeply empathetic, and altruistic in their approach to each other, other people, and life.

This sourceful relationship represents the possibility that a core group can cause a breakthrough in establishing an innovative model, and that model will reflect the imminent arrival of a new paradigm of extraordinary relationships.

The union of two leaders in such a relationship speaks to the power and possibility of having a relationship that transcends relationship as we know it. This emerging model of leader-to-leader relationship is a newfound dynamic that will inspire and empower all relationships.

Women Point, Men Lead, and Women Follow and Manage

When women point, it speaks to a visionary quality consistent with women's innate relationship to past, present, and future. Men are primarily and innately grounded in present time, having a single perspective of here and now.

The ability of women to see down the road and into the future allows them to have an accurate view of what lies ahead. The predictable dynamic of a sourceful relationship points to the emerging paradigm of extraordinary relationships that will impact the planet and transcend the condition of patriarchy.

Here is what the power source relationship looks like: The woman is safe, visionary, complete, and fulfilled. Her love and respect of Self is unconditional. She uncovers a vision of her and her partner's future that is empowering not only for the relationship but for life itself. This is the woman pointing to the future, creating a succinct picture that is realistic and that correlates to the present reality. She is able to decipher the vision in a way that reveals that future as if it actually exists before it has emerged.

Along comes a courageous man. This man is devoted to empowering the woman and her vision. He perceives that vision as one that she is committed to on her own *and* with him as her visionary partner. He is honored to lead and to bring this vision, which is now *their* vision, into existence. His ownership of the vision is the result of powerful leadership, and it deepens their already inspired relationship. He considers the vision to be a co-creation—one that produces a future that was previously unpredictable. This man is filled with a joy and ecstasy that continues to motivate him through the completion. The man is leading with a style and approach that arises from the belief that the vision was his creation as well. This level of ownership empowers the man to deeply appreciate his role in their partnership.

As this vision unfolds, the woman's responsibility shifts to managing her partner as they move into their created future. Guiding his actions in what she continues to perceive as their vision, she takes on a vital role, reflected in their vision being fulfilled. The partners have aligned to a point that the love and commitment they have vowed to each other is alive and growing.

Chapter 19:
The Keys to Everlasting Love

The everlasting stage of a relationship represents a totally different interpretation of what love is. Everlasting relationships transcend the individuals involved, while still authentically acknowledging their contribution. Everlasting relationships draw energy from life as a creation, valuing the service and contribution of the couple beyond any other dynamic. In the end, an everlasting relationship has the possibility to develop into the ideal relationship characterized by the phrase *you are me*.

Most everlasting relationships can be described as "you and me." This powerfully inclusive relationship requires the existence of a narrow space between the two people. The space is the difference between a romantic relationship ("youandme") and an everlasting relationship. The space that partners experience in an everlasting relationship ("you and me") gives both individuals permission to be uniquely themselves while still deeply experiencing the benefits of an inclusive relationship. This extraordinarily empowering relationship allows each individual to create her or his own uniqueness, which exponentially expands within that relationship.

Everlasting relationships are inclusive of others, unlike romantic stages, which are exclusive of others. In an everlasting relationship there is future, past, and present; within it, each partner leads with the future, acknowledges the past, and lives in the present. An everlasting relationship transcends all differences between the partners. Those differences are, in fact, cherished and embraced.

The Five Keys to an Everlasting Relationship

1. Consistent and in-depth communication

This means you speak consistently and powerfully listen to your partner whether you are together or apart. You share key aspects of your life with your partner not just so your partner understands the context of yourself that given day or knows the details of what went on for you but also to generate love, deep appreciation, and profound respect.

In being complete, you are responsible with your communications; in other words, you say all there is to be said. Expressing yourself empathetically, you are aware that what you say may cause an upset that could generate further conversation, but you communicate with an intention to have your partner be complete.

2. A common life purpose and common values

When people get married in the romantic stage, details are often overlooked; this can lead to disagreement or the eventual dissolution of the relationship. It's important to be in alignment on the following critical issues (note that there may be others):

- Sex and monogamy
- Attitude toward children
- Level of education
- Religious issues and differences
- Belief in spirituality
- Expectations of lifestyle and standards of living
- Approach to the future
- Relationship to mortality

3. A healthy approach to conflicts and breakdowns

When you first become committed to one another, you may not have all the skills you need to be able to argue constructively. However over time, the ability to resolve conflict—and to know that there is no argument greater than your commitment to one another—is crucial to establishing an everlasting relationship.

You need to have the capacity to argue constructively, especially when one of you is in trouble, is opposed, or is feeling alone. You will also love and support one another when times are challenging and be able to contribute to and receive from your partner without keeping score.

4. Context for the relationship beyond the relationship itself

Generating an unconditional commitment, together or separately, to something you are both aligned with that is beyond the relationship itself is vital. If you are just focusing on the relationship itself, the minutiae and the day-to-day "stuff" of life will eventually wear you down. The *context* you have that is greater than your own relationship will put all the everyday *content* in perspective and allow you to move forward with your priorities in an easy and powerful way. Your context (or cause) may be philanthropic, charitable, or spiritual, or it may be a dedication to the possibility of making a unique difference in the world.

5. Authentic acknowledgment and profound respect

Without these principles, otherwise loving and committed couples will not experience an everlasting relationship. Men appreciate women who authentically acknowledge the intention to create and build something from nothing. A man's sensitivity in the moment is different than a woman's. Authentically acknowledging a man in what he does—whether it's in the relationship or at work—will empower him. He is in the relationship for more than just what he is doing. From this acknowledgment he learns that his love and commitment is heartfelt and that it surpasses his comprehension of himself. When the acknowledgement comes from a woman, it makes his efforts seem worthwhile. Men appreciate authentic acknowledgment from their partners.

The woman in a relationship is empowered by being profoundly respected. She needs to know her unique contribution is an indelible aspect of the relationship itself. Profound respect, for a woman, is equivalent to being loved. As a woman evolves in a committed relationship, the direct and consistent experience of being profoundly respected by her partner becomes essential. This context allows her to access her innate ability to love and empower.

A Living Example

Christine and Mark came to me for coaching. Christine felt that her husband dismissed her when she tried to talk to him about her issues at work or her issues with her family and friends. She also thought he tried to fix situations without listening to the full story. After explaining authentic acknowledgment and profound respect to the couple, I asked them to practice with each other.

Christine found numerous ways to authentically acknowledge Mark, thanking him when he took out the trash or took the dogs for a walk when she was tired. Then the real change in their relationship occurred. One evening, Christine came home from work and talked about a problem she had at the office. While he made dinner, Mark listened attentively. He began to more than just hear her; he began listening from her perspective instead of giving in to his impulse to fix the situation. When she was done talking about the problem, Mark offered suggestions on how to resolve the problem without diminishing her experience.

For the first time in a long while, Christine felt deeply understood by Mark. Christine experienced being fully heard and respected by her spouse. The interaction was radically different from other conversations, which always seemed to be one-sided or confrontational to Christine, leaving her feeling alone and unappreciated.

Once Mark began to show profound respect for Christine, every aspect of her life was positively impacted. She noticed changes in the time she spent with their son and the time she spent at work. She felt more confident, productive, and playful. Mark continued this way of being with patience and love, and Christine continued authentically acknowledging him. Their relationship was never the same.

That one conversation—and the experience Christine had afterward—created an instantaneous shift in the relationship that has affected how they behave with one another to this day. From the time they wake up in the morning until they close their eyes at night, Mark's profound respect for Christine is always present. This inspires Christine to authentically acknowledge Mark for intimately including her in his life. The way they regard one another has transformed their relationship and deepened their commitment to each other.

Chapter 20:
The New Model for Love

For as long as language has existed, the interpretations and meanings of love have failed to illustrate and illuminate the depth, power, and possibility of love. The essence of love is missing from the global perspective, yet we live in a world that yearns for love. We all want to love and be loved by each other and by the world community.

It would be a pure act of creation in the moment of now for love to exist forever into the future. Love is diluted or lost and not fully appreciated unless created anew in the moment. The memory of love may be appreciated and may even be empowering, and yet the essence of love as an act of creation is immediate and exciting and takes on a life of its own. The process of the creation of love takes on a context of deep affinity, romance, and generosity. This may be expanded to include healing, declarations of peace, and the possibility of a global alignment.

To create love in the moment is different than declaring love into the future. Declaring love into the future may be the means by which we can create love in the moment from an entirely different perspective. For example, when two people get married, they speak the vows and make a commitment "to love and honor in sickness and in health, till death do us part." This declaration, spoken into the future and created in present time, is a creation of love.

The commitment to maintain a lifelong partnership, empowered by a declaration of love into the future, establishes a foundation for the loving relationship. This declaration of infinite and eternal love may be the same declaration that establishes peace among women and men throughout the world.

The words *I love you* may contain more historical baggage and elicit more fear than any other three-word statement. *I love you* seems to powerfully imply that you are obligated to love the other person back. You are expected to say "I love you too."

My definition of a future model of love is this: The love I speak to in my love for you virtually makes me and my identity disappear. All there is, then, is my standing and creating, being completely in your world. Therefore, I have chosen to surrender and to powerfully experience you from a perspective that empowers me to love and be loved by you.

The love story that empowers and inspires the world around this relationship is that future model. This is love personified—the kind of love that can only be shared and given away; the kind of love that creates and builds communities; the kind of love that causes spontaneous acts of freedom, generosity, compassion, and empathy toward oneself and others. This kind of love is an aligned partnership that will impact a critical mass of people. It will cause the new paradigm of extraordinary relationships to flourish.

The context of those simple three words, *I love you,* consistent with this interpretation of love, can occur magically, with no history, baggage, or fear about communicating. This is when it is easy to say *I love you.* An *I love you* that comes from the essence of one human being to another without any reasons, obligations, or inauthenticity is the ultimate expression of love.

In this new model, when two people connect and empower each other through love, the impact goes beyond them. Every interaction they have when not with each other is empowered by their love, sharing and expanding what's possible as a natural expression of one's Self.

The reflections about what love is in its most idyllic form

historically come from artists, musicians, poets, and philosophers. Now you, too, have that creative gift. Your new interpretation of love goes beyond relationships and life as you knew it to be. Coming from your Self, this interpretation creates love as a magical and enchanting possibility.

The end is just your beginning...

Notes to Myself

In Closing and Coaching

I am honored that you have completed reading this book. To know that you have read my words and immersed yourself in my life's work is meaningful to me. That you are engaged in being in an extraordinary relationship with yourself and with others speaks volumes about our collective commitment. Together, we will ensure a future in which all our relationships go beyond what we once believed happiness and reality could be.

Your extraordinary relationships will impact your life and the people you touch with love and new possibilities. The work in front of you need not be difficult. Being aware that we live life in the gap between mediocre and extraordinary is key. Looking upward and into your created future consistently and moment to moment is essential. You will forget sometimes. We all do. Simply observe your lapse and instantly create your extraordinary moment with a smile.

Remember: your way of being is always secondary to you being a human being—that is, be gentle with yourself. Create space for your humanity. If you need to forgive yourself or another, do so. Forgiveness makes an enormous difference. This is all part of you being *extraordinary*.

Your ability to focus on observing your own feminine and masculine energies with no personal judgements is essential. Stay true to this exercise for about one month, and your energies will naturally adjust. You are capable of achieving your breakthrough and having your energies aligned. Soon enough, you will no longer think about it. You will simply be *all* you know yourself to be.

Additional Coaching

As a woman, remember that you are safe, visionary, fulfilled and complete, and you authentically acknowledge your man and all men. As a courageous man, you are fun, certain and clear; you are a lover and generator, and you are always profoundly respectful. **It is within your personal power to transform yourself, your relationships, and your life.**

This book comes to you from my heart and soul and from my future to your future. I am inspired by your openness and receptivity in allowing me the privilege to contribute what passionately lives within me. Please know that this is not mine but ours together. God bless you.

Respectfully,

Martin

Acknowledgments

To my mother, Lillie Calderon Cohen, for her purity of heart and unconditional love: You are forever in my heart. To my father, Harry Cohen, for magnanimously referring to me as his hero: You are forever my hero. To my grandmother Chana Cohen, the personification of power and leadership: You have had an enormous impact on my life.

You are all more alive within me than ever.

To Maureen Martellotto Cohen, my loving wife. You are my gift from God, the source of all that is extraordinary in my life. I would not be at this place if not for you.

To my family, who I adore always; my brother Lenny, may you rest in peace; my brother Maurice; and my sister-in-law Tirzah, I love you and thank you for the profound difference you have made in my life.

To my sons and daughters—Aaron, Shari, Rebecca, Joshua, and Randy—for always contributing to me and giving me everything I need to grow with wisdom. To my amazing grandchildren—Alec, Hannah, and Sandy— for keeping me young at heart.

To the entire Cohen family, I am always inspired by your presence and am blessed to be a part of this extraordinary family.

Friends and contributors, each one of you in your own way has specifically empowered me. You know who you are. I thank specifically Linda Cohen Slezak, Peggy Williams, Dr. Ann Gordon, Will Dunnigan, Jayne Weiss, Penny Spiwack, Dr. Mara Schiff, Harvey Herman, David Bennahum, David Barrett, Ken Wilensky, Vanessa Uzcategui, Jill Franks, Nian Fish, Natane Boudreau, Danielle Posa, Janie Wood, Dr. Jim Valentine, Meg Thompson, Meghan Stevenson, Dr. Alan and Roberta Shader, Howard Wolkowitz, Arthur Goldglantz, Dr. Harvey Austin, Jeff Meschel, and Dr. Daniel Booth Cohen.

Joan Holmes, founding president and CEO of the Hunger Project, I thank you for opening my eyes to a world that I was blind to. I can now see the realistic probability of ending hunger and starvation in our lifetime.

Thanks to Tracey Leigh Carswell, my invaluable associate who never stopped loving and supporting me.

To Virginia Aronson, a master editor, you brought me to clarity and simplicity.

To Miss Rose Port, my ninth-grade teacher who said the magic words, "Martin, don't you ever stop!"

To my mentors: Werner Erhard, an iconic man from my past and of my future, I am forever indebted to you. Dr. Arthur Phillips, my quintessential *mensch*, your spirit, humor, and brilliance are always there for me. Kezia Keeble, the Woman, a trendsetter who showed me the way I will never forget, your insight elicited the best from me; may you rest in peace.

Thanks to Landmark Worldwide and its staff, Program Leaders, and Forum Leaders. Your unyielding commitment to humanity is incomparable and is always delivered with empathy, dignity, and professionalism. To the staff and members of Sukyo Mahikari. My deepest appreciation for bringing my spirituality and the Light to me, my family, and my ancestors. To the Hunger Project, an evolutionary organization committed to ending world hunger and starvation in our lifetime. You are a context for my life, and I am profoundly grateful. Thanks to the team at Balboa Press, especially Adriane Pontecorvo, for providing a literary platform that expands my contribution in the world.

To all the participants in my workshops and seminars, my clients, my staff, and all those who have assisted me. Thank you from the bottom of my heart for your amazing generosity and your contribution to my life's work about women, men, and relationships.

If I missed anyone, please forgive me and know that I deeply appreciate all your love and support!

Made in the USA
San Bernardino, CA
20 January 2018